God Meant It All For Good

ELAINE ROSE

ISBN: 9798407987246

I dedicate this book to Jesus Christ, my
Lord and Saviour

When Joseph's brothers saw that their father was dead, they said, 'What if Joseph holds a grudge against us and pays us back for all the wrongs we did to him?' So they sent word to Joseph, saying, 'Your father left these instructions before he died: "This is what you are to say to Joseph: I ask you to forgive your brothers the sins and the wrongs they committed in treating you so badly." Now please forgive the sins of the servants of the God of your father.' When their message came to him, Joseph wept. His brothers then came and threw themselves down before him. 'We are your slaves,' they said. But Joseph said to them, 'Don't be afraid. Am I in the place of God? You meant to harm me, but God meant it for good to accomplish what is now being done, the saving of many lives.'

Genesis 50:15–20

INTRODUCTION

When God set me free to live the life I have now, I began to tell my story to other women, and the people who heard it would often say, 'Elaine, you should write a book'. My Christian friends always felt that putting my story out in the world for others to read was part of God's plan for my life, and I remember praying, 'Lord, if you want me to write a book, make it possible for me to put my story down, so I can use it to help others.' And after a while, He did.

As I tell you this now, I've been free for eight years, after a whole lifetime of abuse. It's still very painful to think about, and although I now live in joy, thankfulness and hope, there are things about life that I still find difficult. But I've written down my story as best I can, from where I am now, in the hope that it will give strength to other women. If you're going through similar experiences to the things I suffered at the hands of my abusers; if you feel trapped and hopeless and can't see a way out, I want to tell you that there is light at the end of that tunnel. Because, against all the odds, I got free.

There's a lot I can't remember about the things that were done to me. I suspect there are things I'll never remember, because they were just too awful for the mind to hold. For a lot of years I questioned God, saying, 'Why me?' But now, when I look at the person I am today, I think, 'Why *not* me?' My experiences have given me strength and humility, and have also given me an understanding that, sadly, I know I share with millions of other women across the world.

All I ever wanted was my freedom, and it was such a long time coming, and such a hard road. But I got there, through the grace of God and the power of prayer. So whoever you are, reading this, I want you to know that no matter what you're going through, you can get free. No matter how many attempts you need to make, and how many setbacks you face; no matter how many people are determined to trap or destroy you, *you can get free.*

And you can heal.

> I hope my story helps you.
>
> With love,
>
> Elaine Rose
>
> Scotland, January 2022.

All the events described in this book are true, but names and some details of place have been changed to protect members of my family.

Search me, God, and know my heart; test me and know my anxious thoughts. See if there is any offensive way in me, and lead me in the way everlasting.

Psalm 139:23–5

PROLOGUE: THE BLACK MARIA

It's the mid-1960s in the north-east of Scotland, and we're in the back of the police van: me, my little sister Laura, and the police. I must have been six at the time, which would make Laura five. It's winter; it's been snowing, though we can't see that as all the windows are blacked out. But I can still hear the *click, click, click* of the press photographer's camera, fading into the distance as we pull away.

'The Black Maria' was what everyone called police vans in those days: they are huge and forbidding, painted pitch-black all over, with hard benches in the back for prisoners. This one's cold as it rattles through the streets of Inverness, but for all the disorientation and discomfort of the journey, it doesn't feel like a bad thing that's happening. It's a relief maybe, or at least some progress. We're being driven to the police station.

The strangest thing about being in the back of the Black Maria is that my mum's here too. She's been gone for well over a year, and I'd started to think I'd never see her again. But she's not here to rescue us, our long-lost mum. She's shouting, 'I don't want them. I can't take care of them. Take them and do what you like with them.'

She looks straight at me and Laura and says, 'I don't want you.'

~ ~ ~

Part One

For you created my inmost being; you knit me together in my mother's womb. I praise you because I am fearfully and wonderfully made; your works are wonderful, I know that full well. My frame was not hidden from you when I was made in the secret place, when I was woven together in the depths of the earth. Your eyes saw my unformed body; all the days ordained for me were written in your book before one of them came to be.

Psalm 139:13–16

~1~

That moment in the Black Maria wasn't the first time my mother had abandoned me. But for her to suddenly reappear, only to look me straight in my little six-year-old face and reject me outright, was a shock. Even so, by that point it wasn't the worst thing to have happened in my young life. Not by a long way.

Details of my earliest childhood are vague. We lived in the Scottish Highlands, in a network of little streets near the ferry port in the city of Inverness. It's a beautiful part of the world but, like everywhere, the Highlands had its dark side of poverty, addiction and violence, and Inverness was no exception.

At first we all lived together: me, my mum and dad, my little sister Laura and my two elder brothers. My eldest brother James was nine years older than me, and Jason was two years older. My parents had had children before – two little boys called David and Andrew, but they had both died in infancy before James was born.

Number 42 North Drive was a small, gable end house. You came in from the side, to a staircase that led up to two bedrooms and a living room and then, along the corridor, another bedroom and the toilet. I can remember the rooms well enough, but I can't remember seeing much of my parents at all. I know my dad was there, but he's just a shadowy figure in my memory. I can't see his face, nor my mum's. I can't even remember my brothers in the house, it's all such a dark haze.

When I try to remember, some images emerge sharp and clear, though they're scenes that I can never quite understand or piece together. There was one night, I must have been very young then, when my parents were doing what was called a moonlight flit –

leaving the house in the middle of the night. To this day I've no idea why, but they suddenly packed all their furniture into a van in the dark of the night and we drove south. My dad came from somewhere in the Dundee area, and it's likely that's where we ended up, a hundred and fifty miles from Inverness. By morning, we'd arrived at this strange new house. I remember a scary man who used to sit on a chair outside the house, smoking a pipe and spitting. Apparently we were there for a while – wherever 'there' was. Long enough for me to go to school, anyway. Apart from the spitting man, my only other memories are of playing in the fields with Laura, and getting into trouble for stealing eggs. Anyhow, after a little while, we all moved back and settled in Inverness again. Except by then, my parents were no longer together.

I have a vivid memory of my mum leaving the house to go somewhere, and me crying, running after her. She was wearing black gloves, and she wiped my nose. I was begging to go with her, but she wouldn't take me. That was the day she disappeared.

~ ~ ~

~2~

Almost straight away, my dad took up with someone else: a busty, fattish, blondish woman called Ada Stevenson. She had a house at Madras Street, not far from where we lived, down along the Ness estuary. It was an old-looking house at the time, and it's been knocked down now. It was very small. There was a living room with a door off to one big bedroom, and through that a door to a tiny box room in the corner, where Laura and I were put. The box room had a square window which banged open and shut in the wind through the night – *bam, bam, bam* – a sound that echoes in my mind even now.

We all lived in that tiny house: me, Laura, my two brothers, Dad and Ada Stevenson. It was a house full of alcohol and noise, with fighting, screaming and bawling through the night, people always coming and going, strangers climbing in through the box room window, people having sex. As a young child, I saw a lot of sex.

For me and Laura, life was dominated by Ada Stevenson, who abused us without mercy. She'd beat us for no reason at all, with brushes, brooms, mop-handles and shoes. She used to wear those wooden-soled sandals called Scholls, which she'd take off and use to clobber us around the head. At night, she'd put us to bed without food or water – she'd just throw us onto the mattress on the floor of the box room, shut the door and leave us there. I remember my throat hurting so much with thirst I couldn't sleep. We were always scared and tired and hungry.

She had a coal fire which she'd keep burning all night long, then make us clean the fireplace out in the morning while it was still hot. I remember my wee hands were always burned, and so were my sister's.

Then, early in the morning, we'd have to take the heavy rugs out and beat them, even while it was still dark.

The figure of my father is there in the background, but he was nearly always away. He was working, I assume, though I don't really know. I remember one morning he had come back, and he was dressing me for school. I couldn't lift my arm up to put it into the sleeve of the blouse because Ada Stevenson had beaten my arm so badly. I think it may have been broken. And I remember this woman Ada standing behind my dad, looking right at me and making a fist, as if to say 'if you tell, there'll be more of this for you'. But my father never questioned anything; he didn't even seem to notice. He put the blouse on me and then he had to go to work, so we were left alone with Ada Stevenson again. Straight away, she made me fill the kettle, and when it boiled she took me over to where the kettle was and poured the boiling water over my hand. And then I ran – straight out of the house to the neighbours across the road, screaming at the top of my lungs, holding my hand out to them. The neighbours took me to hospital in Inverness and had me bandaged me up, and then took me back over to Ada Stevenson's house. I'd told the neighbours that she'd done that to my hand, and perhaps they said something to her about it – but in any case, things just carried on exactly as before.

My Auntie Joan lived at West Drive with her husband James – it was walking distance from Madras Street, but a long walk for a little child. Ada Stevenson soon got into the habit of sending me down to my auntie's with a note asking for food and money. I'd take the note, my auntie would give me some food, and I'd take that back. And then again, a few days later, she'd send me back to my auntie's with a note. In the end Auntie Joan got pretty upset with this. 'Why is she sending you?' she'd ask, exasperated. 'Why does she keep writing these notes asking me for food?' Well, I didn't know, and I couldn't tell her what was going on in that house.

Sexual abuse was a constant presence when I was little: it seemed there was always an uncle or stranger trying to abuse us. When we stayed with my Auntie Pat, Laura slept in the same bed with her and her husband Joseph, and later told me Joseph would spend all night trying to take her pants off in the bed. Another time my Auntie Margaret, my father's sister who had Down's Syndrome and lived at home with my granddad, invited me up to her bedroom and immediately started piling all the furniture up against the door. It felt like she was getting ready to do something to me, but one of my aunties came up, shouting at her to move the furniture away, as though she knew what was about to happen.

There was an Uncle John who used to diddle Laura and me on his knee and always wanted to touch us where he shouldn't. My Auntie Joan was constantly trying to keep him away from us, and years later, when I was a grown woman, she'd tell me, 'Don't ever let him near your kids.'

I learned something else from Joan which helped me to make sense of the family picture: my grandfather – my father's father – was an abuser. When I was visiting her as an adult one time, she suddenly said, 'You know when you were little, Elaine, you stayed with me and your grandfather?'

'No, I don't remember anything about it,' I said.

'We had a big garden out the back,' she told me, 'and I was calling you for your dinner, but I couldn't see you. Then, when I looked out of the window a second time, I saw you with my dad – he had you by the hand, and he was taking you to the shed at the bottom of the garden.'

'Why would he be taking me to the shed?'

'You don't want to know what he was taking you there for,' said Joan. 'It would destroy your life if you knew. You'd never live with yourself. But I caught you in time.'

This was disturbing enough, but it also chimed with something my brother James told me, which is that when my parents were still together this grandfather offered my mum a large sum of money to go away and not come back, and to leave us kids behind. Maybe my mum had seen these things and my granddad was afraid she would report it? Or maybe it was something else. In any case, I have no idea whether she took the money or not.

The constant beatings, the work Ada Stevenson made us do, the deprivation and random acts of extreme cruelty, the physical, mental and sexual abuse . . . it just went on and on, and it all blurs together in my mind. But one event sticks out – the one which I think had the biggest effect on me in later years.

It was night; there were a lot of people in the house as usual. She tied me to a bed, hands and feet. She stuffed my mouth with toilet paper. Then she did the same to Laura, and she left us there in the dark. Then someone – a woman – came in with a big sheet over her head, and stood over us, menacing us and shouting, 'I'm the devil and I'm going to get you. I'm going to kill you!'

From that moment right up until God set me free, my life was dominated by fear. I was constantly fearful; terrified of the dark; convinced that something was always coming to hurt me.

Worst of all was what I learned later from Joan about this. She told me the woman in the sheet was my Auntie Pat – her own sister – who, all through our early childhood, had been complicit in Ada Stevenson's abuse of me and Laura.

~~~

~3~

Ada Stevenson got pregnant. I don't know for sure, but I'm pretty certain from things I've heard down the years that my eldest brother James was sleeping with her when my dad was away – he would have been fifteen at the time – and it seems likely the baby was James's. After the birth, Ada Stevenson stopped Laura from going to school so she could look after the baby, change it and feed it with a bottle, even though at that time my little sister was hardly more than a baby herself.

I still went to school, though often my whole body was black and blue with bruises. Never the face, though, she only ever beat us on our bodies. One day it was PE and I refused to strip down to my kit. The teacher got angrier and angrier, but I wouldn't do it because I was so ashamed. I think I was also protecting my wee sister, for fear of what Ada Stevenson would do to her if the teachers found out what was going on.

The teacher was ordering me to take my clothes off, and I was saying I couldn't, and in the end I told her it was because I was really hurt and sore. So she took me to the school nurse, who took one look at my body and said she was calling the police – but before she could do it, I ran. I ran out of the school, through the gates and into the streets – it was freezing cold at the time, there was snow on the ground, and I had no idea where I was running to – I just knew that I couldn't go back to that house, and if the police got involved, things would only get worse for us. So I wandered around in the cold, and I was so hungry, and so upset thinking about my wee sister and what Ada Stevenson might be doing to her, that eventually I went to one of my aunts. By the time I got to her house I was sobbing uncontrollably.

'What's wrong?' said my auntie.

'My body, my body,' was all I could say.

So she took me and stripped me, bathed me in the kitchen sink and contacted my Auntie Joan. Then once I was dressed again, Auntie Joan said, 'Right, come on, we're going to her.'

They took me to the house on Madras Street and Joan started beating Ada Stevenson – I remember Joan was pregnant at the time, but she was just so angry. They were fighting with their fists, throwing things, screaming. And then Joan saw Laura and looked at her body too, and right away she went to the nearest call box and phoned the police.

Who knows how it would have ended if she hadn't. I've always called Auntie Joan my saviour, as I've no doubt Ada Stevenson would have been capable of murdering us two girls.

Soon the police arrived at the house, along with the social services, and a man called Mr Murray, who everyone called 'the cruelty man' (he was the local government official in charge of cases of child abuse and neglect). They must have asked us questions – this part is all a blur — but I remember Joan pointing to Ada Stevenson and saying, 'It was her, this woman here.'

Then the photographer from the *Inverness Courier* turned up, and took pictures of our bodies — that *click, click, click* haunts me to this day — and then somehow my mum arrived on the scene, and we were loaded into the back of the Black Maria, and the terror and suffering of life at Madras Street was over.

~ ~ ~

Part Two

I'm nobody's child

I'm nobody's child

Just like the flowers

I'm growing wild

No mommy's kisses

And no daddy's smile

Nobody wants me

I'm nobody's child.

No mommy's arms to hold me

Or soothe me when I cry

Sometimes it gets so lonely

I wish that I could die . . .

'Nobody's Child', written by Mel Foree and Cy Coben,
recorded by Karen Young, 1969.

~4~

We didn't stay long at the police station: since our mum had made it so clear that she didn't want anything to do with me or Laura, the next stop for the Black Maria was Scotscraig orphanage on the other side of Inverness.

The big, black iron gates at the bottom of the orphanage drive were closed, so the police had to get out and open them, and in the fading winter light I caught my first glimpse of a huge red sandstone house with ornate windows, rows of chimneys and a massive front doorway like the mouth of a cave, looming at the top of a long, sloping tarmac drive, surrounded by trees and lawn. We were driven up to the entrance, and the police opened the back doors of the van to let us out.

Laura and I stood there, holding hands, just gazing up at the biggest building we'd ever seen – and just as I was starting to feel really frightened, the matron came out and ushered us inside. Having done their job of delivering us the police left, and Mum came with us into the matron's office.

When it became clear that Mum was definitely leaving us there, Laura and I got terribly upset – I remember howling and crying, and Mum saying, 'I'll be back for you. I'll call tomorrow.' But she never did call, and she never came to take us away, and it was a long time before I saw her again.

As this was going on, the matron was writing down our details in a big book. Then, once Mum had gone, she took us through one of the doors in her office into a huge store cupboard full of all kinds of clothing, as well as boots, shoes and coats, and she picked out sets of clothes for us. After that she led us down long corridors lined with thick, brown-painted doors, into a bathroom with rows of little kiddie-sized sinks and toilets and a big bath. Then a dormitory with nine beds: my bed was by the door and Laura would be three beds along. Then the tour took us back down to the front door with its big bell and stained-glass panel above like a church, through endless corridors of bare, cream-painted walls with a wooden rail halfway up, and polished red concrete floors. Past the dining room, the kitchen, the boot-cleaning room, up dark-carpeted stairs with shiny, brown-painted banisters to more toilets and bedrooms. It was an old, old building, and all very brown.

That night we had a bath with a hard, stinky bar of soap and went to bed in our cotton orphanage pyjamas, in fresh white sheets with heavy, yellowish woolly blankets on top. We were scared and sad, but for the first time we could remember, we were also clean, well-fed and safe.

~ ~ ~

~5~

After the chaos of Madras Street, life in the orphanage was amazingly orderly. There were so many kids there – babies right up to teenagers – and each age group had a set bathtime and bedtime. Everyone ate meals in the dining room together, with the little ones in their highchairs. Breakfast was porridge, toast and tea on school days and cornflakes at the weekend; dinner was usually mince or some other kind of meat, with potatoes and green peas – except on a Friday, which was always fish and chips. There was never a choice, you had to eat what you were given – though I got very good at hiding fish in a napkin down my trousers and flushing it down the toilet afterwards. I hated the fish!

There were puddings and custard, and at the weekends, teatime treats like scrambled eggs on toast or mashed banana sandwiches. Mealtimes were strict – you had to be quiet, and no one was allowed to leave the table until everyone had finished – but the food was decent, and we never went hungry. If I ever catch the smell of milky tea in a plastic beaker, it always brings back happy memories of meals at the orphanage.

Mondays to Fridays were school, Sunday was church, and on Saturdays we'd go outside straight after breakfast to play until dinnertime. The grounds outside were huge, and down at the bottom there were trees with tree-houses and play areas in between, and we'd run and climb and make dens and pull each other around on little bogies.

We had different sets of clothes for every occasion – play clothes, church clothes, party clothes – and at the beginning of every school year we'd be taken into town to buy a new school uniform of grey skirt and cardigan, white blouses, blue blazer and tie and black shoes, and a new school bag. And we were given pocket money for treats, too.

I liked all the staff at the orphanage, but my absolute favourites were Dolly and Auntie Jay. Dolly was the cook, and she was just lovely – I was always happy when it was my turn to help her with the washing-up. She was very tall, and had a huge pantry off the kitchen, stacked with tins of all the scones and cakes she baked. She took a real shine to Laura, and used to be allowed to take Laura home with her for weekends sometimes, as we had no one to visit us or take us out. Then there was Jay, who we always called 'Auntie'. She was very young and pretty, with short blonde hair, and I remember her ironing all the kids' clothes in the playroom while keeping an eye on us. Sometimes Auntie Jay lived in at the orphanage, and she'd take some of us up to her room – she had lots of bottles of perfume all lined up, and she'd squirt a bit on us. The staff used to smoke in the bedroom, and that mix of cigarette smoke and perfume is another smell that brings back good memories.

Every week, we went to something called Children's Happy Hour, run by a Christian man called Martin. I'll never forget him; he was so nice to me. The first day I went there, Martin said, 'Kids, if you can memorize the names of the books of the Bible for next week, you'll get a gift.' A gift! This was really exciting! Back at the orphanage I ran to tell Matron, and she told me to get my Bible out and see what I could do. I memorized loads of them. So the next Tuesday, I went back and Martin said, 'Is there anyone who's memorized the names?' and my hand shot up – me! There were only two of us, and I'd memorized the most. 'Wow,' said Martin, 'you've done really well.' And he gave me a pencil and a rubber that said *Jesus Loves You* on it. The Children's Happy Hour was my first positive experience of Christianity, and it would be a big influence on me in years to come.

Christmases and birthdays at the orphanage were wonderful – we had birthday parties and presents, and at Christmas Santa would come, and lots of important people from the city would visit. I remember there was always a girl dressed up as a princess who would come to the orphanage, and once she let me put her tiara on my head. At this time, my dream was to be a nurse when I grew up. I told all the people who visited, all my teachers and anyone else who would listen, that I was going to be a nurse. So for birthdays and Christmas I was given nurse's uniforms and toy nurse's kits, and I'd play at nursing all the other children.

Every summer, they took us all for two weeks' holiday to Rosemarkie – a little village on the Black Isle with a beautiful beach, just up the coast from Inverness. We stayed in a huge house, and played on the beach every day. I remember we used to go to the farm to get the milk in a silver churn, and a friendly sheep called Fiona would come up to the fence and let you pet her. But the thing I remember most about the holidays was messing around with my wee pal and partner-in-mischief, Victor. Victor was a cheeky, fat little boy, with red hair and freckles like me. He was always smiling, and he was always up to something. At the orphanage, me and Victor used to climb over the wall to nick apples from the neighbour's garden, and it was Victor who first discovered the scary secret passage from the orphanage gardens, which went into the cellar and up to the children's bathroom. I Victor him years later, when we were grown up, and we still laughed about the time I shut him in the boot of Matron's car in Rosemarkie because he'd slapped me on my sunburn.

All this time, I had no idea where my brothers were. But I had my little sister – we were hardly ever apart. And all in all, orphanage life was pretty good.

~ ~ ~

~6~

One Saturday, Laura and I were playing down at the bottom of the orphanage grounds. I was pushing her on an old set of pram wheels, and we were on our way round to my favourite tree, the Giant Tree, to see if we could hear the cuckoo that used to sit in it. As I pushed her out onto the path, I saw there were two women out by the big iron gates, and I heard one of them say, 'Hello.' It seemed like she was talking to me, so I pushed Laura over there and looked through the gate, holding on to the bars.

'Who are you?' I said to one of them; a brown-haired lady.

'I'm your mother,' she said.

I said, 'I don't have a mother.'

She said, 'I'm your mother, and this is your auntie,' pointing at the other lady. Then she said, 'You're Laura.'

'I'm not Laura!' I said, indignantly, and pointed at my wee sister. 'She's Laura.'

'You're Elaine, then.'

Oh, I thought. She knows my name. And it was strange, because there were times in the orphanage when I'd felt so lonely, and just wanted more than anything for my mum or my dad to come – but now that this woman was here saying she was my mum, I felt nothing. There was nothing about her that I recognised. There was just no bond; no urge to be near her. More than anything, I felt frightened.

So Laura and I turned tail and ran all the way up to the orphanage, calling out for Matron – 'Matron, matron! There's a woman here says she's our mother!'

Matron took us inside and then went down to bring the two women (who really were my mum and her sister) up into her office. I have no idea what was said, but Matron must have asked them to leave – and that, I thought, was that.

~~~

~7~

'I hate you, I hate you!'

A few Saturdays later, I'm sitting on a wooden bench in the Castle Restaurant in Inverness, just down the hill from the orphanage. Next to me is Laura, who's keeping very quiet. Opposite us is our mum and her new husband, and beside us is the waitress.

'I hate you, I hate you! I don't want you and I don't want anything to eat!'

That's me, yelling my head off. The husband's keeping quiet too, and the waitress is patiently waiting for our order, but I just can't stop shouting.

'I don't want anything from you!'

Somehow, Mum's managed to get permission to take us out, and suddenly I don't feel nothing when I look at her. What I feel now is furious. Raging! All I want to do is punish this woman who'd abandoned us, rejected us; who had never been there to protect us from all the abuse we'd suffered.

'I hate you!'

The quiet husband goes off somewhere and comes back with a shiny watch, which he dangles in front of me – to try and distract or pacify me, I suppose.

'I don't want your stupid watch! I hate you!'

At this, Mum snaps. 'That's enough of that behaviour!' She's been drinking – she and the husband are both alcoholics – and she doesn't have a clue what to do with me and my anger. She just can't handle it. So she jumps up, grabs me and Laura, and pushes us all past the waitress and out onto the street. None of us gets any lunch that day.

Then, on the way back up the steep hill to the orphanage, my dad suddenly appears, and starts arguing with Mum, right on the street, while the new husband just stands there watching them shout at each other. Then, just as suddenly, the argument's over. Dad carries on down the hill, and Mum turns round, grabs us, and marches us back to the orphanage.

I won't see my mum again for nearly forty years.

~~~

~8~

For the next year or so, life at the orphanage continued as happily as before. But then – and to this day, I have no way of explaining or understanding how this could possibly be the case – Ada Stevenson got a job there.

Even writing this down feels bizarre. As far as I've been able to find out, she was arrested the day we were taken away from Madras Street and was later sectioned (detained in a psychiatric hospital) – so she couldn't possibly have been considered fit to work in an orphanage. But I know from talking to Mrs Francis the matron in later life that mistakes could be made, and background checks for new staff weren't always thorough.

However it happened, one day I was walking down the corridor and glimpsed a woman coming out of Matron's office, and when I turned to see who it was, every part of my body froze. I recognised her immediately: same fattish figure, same blondish hair. I can't remember if I met her eye, but I could feel that she saw me, and I started trembling uncontrollably, shaking all over, still rooted to the spot. This must have only lasted for seconds, but the shockwaves running through my body were so intense it felt like hours. Eventually, I managed to get out of that corridor.

I couldn't say anything, though. The thought of that woman gripped me with such terror I was unable to speak about it, to Matron or anyone.

Ada's job was like Auntie Jay's: ironing the clothes, watching us in the playroom, getting us into the dining room for our lunch, that kind of thing. And at first, she didn't acknowledge me or Laura – she treated us just like the rest, and acted like she didn't know us. But there was always a look about her that chilled me to the bone. She knew that we knew. Once again, I was living in fear.

One night, as she was putting me to bed, she threw up the covers and thrust me roughly onto the mattress. I remember saying 'Please, please, please, please. There's a bogeyman under the bed. Please will you look, will you look?' I was scared of everything again, just as I was at Madras Street.

'There's nobody under the bed,' she said, and she turned off the light and slammed the door shut. I was petrified of the dark, and always slept with a wee light on. But she left me in the dark, and I don't know if I was dreaming, but I thought I could hear a storm outside. I knew the window and the curtains were closed, but it felt like the storm was coming in. Suddenly, I was wide awake – the window and curtains were open, and someone was trying to strangle me. I remember struggling and trying to scream – then nothing. And when I woke up in the morning, there were scrapes and scratches on my hands and arms.

I tried to tell someone, but I couldn't get the words out – I was gasping and gabbling that something had happened – the window – someone had come in, but they said it couldn't have happened. It must have been a nightmare. Could I have scratched myself in my sleep? But I'd felt it: someone's hands on my throat, trying to strangle me. The next night Ada Stevenson put me to bed again, and I was screaming. Matron came to calm me down and reassure me there was no one in the bed and no one could get into the room, but I knew. And the next day, there were footprints from the balcony outside the window, leading right up to my bed. Deep down, I knew it was her. Maybe she was afraid I'd tell Matron about her past. The orphanage must have investigated, because of the footprints, but the staff still tried to reassure me that nothing could have happened, and Ada Stevenson kept her job.

Soon after that, Matron went away on a long weekend, leaving Ada on duty, and that's when her reign of terror began. Straight away on the Friday evening she started the abuse, turning off all the lights to frighten the kids. Laura and I, we knew what she was capable of, and we were terrified. Then she took us into the garden in the dark and made us eat dirt and worms, and she was hitting us – me and Laura, and some of the other kids as well. Then she took me into the orphanage on my own, stripped me naked, ran a bath of ice-cold water, threw me into that bath, and held me down, under the water.

I remember struggling desperately and almost fainting, and the water going everywhere. Eventually, she pulled me out and stood me on the floor, shivering. Even to this day I make a strange gasping noise, and I've been told by doctors that this is most likely the traumatic effect of being thrown into that ice-cold bath of water by someone who was trying to drown me. Eventually she dried me and then threw me – literally threw me through the air – into the playroom.

I don't know what she did to any of the other children, and I hate to think, but later that night when some of the kids had been put to bed and some were still up, including me and Laura, she switched off all the lights again – every light in the place. It was terrifying.

All of this continued the next day, and the next – but thankfully, Matron decided to come back early from her long weekend, so we were rescued on the Sunday night. She must have noticed something was wrong as she was coming up the drive, and she burst through the door asking questions. 'What on earth is going on here?' 'Why are all the lights off?' But we children were too afraid to say anything. Then on the Monday morning, we were all called into the office: me, Laura, and a few of the other children. And we all came forward and told Matron what Ada Stevenson had been doing. I have no idea what Ada herself said when she was called into the office, but she was never seen in the orphanage again.

~ ~ ~

~9~

Not long after this, Laura and I had another visitor from the past: our dad reappeared. I learned later from Mrs Francis the matron that he'd been phoning for some time, asking if he could see us and take us out for a day; protesting his innocence in our abuse, and promising he could be trusted. Social services were consulted, and eventually permission was given, and one Saturday, he got to take us out.

From what I can remember, Dad was OK – he bought us some clothes and shoes and then took us for lunch. But he was an alcoholic and he was drinking, and while we were having our lunch in a restaurant he got drunk and just fell asleep right there at the table. The staff tried to wake him, but we knew better, and were old enough to ask them just to take us back to the orphanage. So the police were called to take us back, and that was the last I saw of my dad for a long time.

I started feeling that the orphanage – a place of order and safety, caring adults and happy times – had been thoroughly ruined for me. I was around ten years old by this time, and I was beginning to understand a few things, and I was angry. My wee pal Victor, for all his chubby smiles, was a very unhappy child too. He used to run away a lot, and I started to join him. This wasn't like our old mischief: I really wanted to get out of there.

First we waited till the staff were on their coffee break, then Victor kept watch in the corridor while I sneaked into the office and took a few pounds from the bureau where they kept the petty cash and our pocket money, making sure to fasten the purses and close the bureau up tightly afterwards. Then we crept down the corridor to the big brown door with the stained glass at the top. Opened it a fraction, squeezed through, shut it slowly, slowly, so as not to make a sound. Walk down the path as though you're not up to anything at all, carefully up onto the stone wall at the side of the huge black iron gates, and pop over the wooden fence there.

Then 'Come on!' and we're on the pavement, running as fast as we can, past all the big posh houses, all the way down the hill to the traffic lights. There's a hotel on the corner by the traffic lights but we're going left, the other way, down the brae, a mile to town. I remember how good it felt walking down with Victor, holding hands, swinging our arms, going around the town, getting some sweets. Just for a while, not a care in the world. We did it a couple of times, and I loved it.

Of course we got caught soon enough – one of the folks in the posh houses would have seen us going over the fence if the orphanage staff hadn't already noticed we were missing. We were picked up by police, which scared us a bit, and taken back to the home, where we owned up to stealing, agreed to pay it back out of our pocket money, and promised not to run away again.

Punishments weren't harsh at the orphanage – a quick smack on the hand or bottom, then straight out to play.

~~~

~10~

After the shock of Ada Stevenson, the disappointment of Dad's reappearance, and the failure of my escape attempts with Victor, things settled down again. Life at the orphanage was still good. I had school and church and holidays and treats. And I had Laura, and we were safe from harm, which is how it should have been.

But as I got older there was another incident which showed how precarious the orphanage's grip on our safety really was, no matter how hard they tried. There was a guy called Mr Jones, who was well respected in the town, and used to come to the orphanage on a Sunday to take some of us to the swimming pool. He'd take the older girls: me, Laura,

Roseanna and Jennifer, Karen and Brenda. Six of us. When we got to the swimming pool, he'd always find a way of singling one of us out – he'd say, 'you don't need to go swimming today, you can sit up here on the balcony and watch the rest of the girls,' and he'd sit us on his knee and diddle us, and get an erection. I remember feeling his erection on my bum and trying to jump off his knee, but he held me too tight. Then, when we got into the pool, he'd come in too, and touch us all over our legs.

When he brought us back to the orphanage, the six of us would talk about what he'd done – we all felt sick and frightened, and we knew we should tell Matron. Then one Sunday, he was doing the same things, putting his hands all over us. And Jennifer – she must have been about eleven at this point – said, 'If you don't stop that, we're going to tell the matron.' That gave us the courage we needed. When he took us home that day, we all spoke to Matron, and that was the end of swimming trips with Mr Jones. Many years later, I gave evidence against him at a child abuse enquiry.

For all the bumps in the road, the orphanage was still a good place for me. It was the only home I'd ever known, and I always felt looked after. I was often lonely, and I knew there were things missing from my life, but Laura and I were inseparable and the happy times – parties, holidays, Christmases and treats – were just wonderful. I have so many fond memories.

I kept in touch with Mrs Francis, the Matron, right up to her death. We'd write letters to each other, and talk on the phone. She once told me that she was married and had a son but her husband and son were taken in a car accident. She always said she believed God gave her the position in the orphanage and the children there to care for. As a Christian now, I believe that God placed those good people in the lives of children who were abandoned, unloved and damaged. For me, the orphanage was my family, all the kids there were my brothers and sisters, and the staff – who really loved and cared for us – were my true parents.

But then, once I was a teenager, I had to leave it all behind.

~~~

Part Three

Father forgive them, for they know not what they do.

Matthew 23:34

~11~

Laura and I were sent a hundred and fifty miles away to the Convent of the Good Shepherd in Edinburgh, a city we'd never been to, where we knew nobody. The convent has since been demolished, but was a huge, forbidding building out near Redford Barracks in the suburb of Colinton.

We shared a little room, me and my sister. It was just a tiny cubicle really, four walls with no ceiling, and it was miserable. Everything in the convent was about rules and obedience and punishment. There were no treats, no outings, no playtimes. It was school on a weekday, Mass on a Sunday, and that was it. I hated the church at that time.

The only light in the darkness was a lady called Jean Love who sometimes came to do arts and crafts with us. She used to bring me sweets. 'You're a lovely girl, Elaine,' she said to me once, 'I really like you.' And I remember crying and crying at the thought that someone liked me. She'd try to persuade me to behave, but all I wanted to do was rebel.

My teenage mind was overwhelmed with questions: Who am I? Why am I here? Why is this happening? Where's my mum? Where's my dad? Why does nobody want me? I used to wonder what I had done to deserve all this. I'd blame myself, because I didn't have any other answers.

Back when Laura and I were first sent to the orphanage in Inverness, my dad took my eldest brother James and ran away with him. Social services were trying to take James into care as well, but Dad wouldn't give him up to the system. Apparently there were appeals on TV for sightings of this missing boy, but no one ever reported seeing him. They went on the run, James and my dad, sleeping in train carriages and on buses – though I didn't find any of this out until I was an adult.

What I did discover, after I arrived at the Convent of the Good Shepherd, was that our other brother, Jason, had also been taken into care and was at a boys' home somewhere near Portobello, about ten miles away on the other side of Edinburgh. I started running away from the convent to look for him. One day I found the place. I asked for him, and he came out. I didn't have many memories of him from childhood so it wasn't a particularly emotional reunion, but it did feel wonderful to have found my brother. I told him I was at the convent, but that I'd run away. He said 'Elaine, you can't run away, you have to go back. You can't be running away, it's not safe. Go back to the convent.' So I went back, and I didn't go to visit him again after that. But I didn't stop running away, either.

One morning, just as I was about to leave for school, I thought, 'I don't want to go to school'. The nuns made us wear horrible, shabby dresses to school, and I hated those dresses more than anything. I was sick of wearing them. So I took my own clothing in my school bag, and a little way down the road I took off my convent dress and put my own clothes on. And I went downtown in Edinburgh, just wandering about, on and off the buses, in shops, sometimes pinching the occasional sweetie to eat. I was careful to get back into my tatty dress in time to go on the bus with the other girls back to the convent, and I was sure I'd got away with it. But just as I was walking down the path, Sister Consolata tapped on the office window and gestured for me to come in.

'How was school today, Elaine?'

'Oh, it was great. I loved the science class.'

'You're lying,' she said. 'I got a call from the school to say you weren't there.'

And she pulled back her hand and slapped me hard in the face. It was sudden, and horribly painful, and before I could stop myself, I'd cursed and swore at Sister Consolata. She grabbed me, dragged me to my room, and started ripping my posters off the walls (I remember I had a lot of posters of the pop star David Essex at the time. He was my hero). She said, 'Gather all your stuff. You're not staying here with your sister anymore.'

And that just drove me crazy. 'You can't take me away from my sister!' I screamed. 'You can't do that to me!' Laura and I had never been separated. But she dragged me out, and threw me into a huge empty room with a stone floor. It looked like a laundry room. No bed, no blankets, no food, nothing – just a bare stone room.

'You'll sleep here tonight,' she said, and shut the door.

With the door closed, I couldn't see anything. The darkness was total – pure black. I felt around and found the door, and I banged and banged on that door, screaming, 'Let me out of here! Let me out!' I was still terrified of the dark. But there was no response from the other side. Just silence.

Eventually I was exhausted, and fell asleep on the freezing stone floor. In the morning, I saw a little light under the door, and heard a key in the lock, and it was Sister Consolata again.

'That was your punishment,' she said. 'Now go and have a shower and have your breakfast and get to school'.

From that day, I was moved to another part of the convent, separated from Laura.

After that I started running away from the convent all the time, me and another girl, but we always got caught. Just a little way down the road, the police car would come.

'Girls, where are you going at this time in the morning?'

'Oh,' we'd say, 'we're going to work.'

'Are you sure you're not from the convent up the road there?'

'Oh, no, no, not at all,' we'd say.

But they knew, and they'd take us in the police car and bring us back to the convent. And the nuns would beat me, slapping and hitting me, throwing things at me.

The nuns knew I was terrified of the dark, and they'd make me take the bins out down a long alleyway at the side of the convent. I'd be shaking at the thought of that bin alley, having flashbacks of Ada Stevenson – I was convinced the devil was going to get me if I went down there. But the nuns forced me. I'd walk down, rigid with fear, looking behind me all the time, then, once I'd put the bin at the end of the alley, I'd run all the way back up as fast as I could.

The years at the convent dragged by. I was petrified of the nuns and bored of everything else, and I hated being separated from Laura. My wee sister was all I had in the world, and I'd always looked out for her. It was my place to care for her, and I felt even more lost without her. In the mornings, when all the girls used the big communal bathrooms before school, I'd see Laura, and she'd be crying. I begged her to tell me what was wrong, but she wouldn't. Then one morning I went to the bathroom and she was in there, just sobbing her heart out. I begged her again, 'Has somebody hurt you? You need to tell me – I can help you.'

But she was too frightened. Eventually, she told me she was being sexually abused and threatened by one of the other girls. I went ballistic at this girl, promising I'd do all manner of harm to her if she ever laid a finger on my sister again. I know the nuns overheard me, though I doubt anything was done about it.

I just wanted to get out of that convent.

~ ~ ~

~12~

When I was around fifteen and a half, just a few months from turning sixteen, I was finally allowed to leave the convent. It wasn't much of an occasion; there were no farewells. Cold as ever, Sister Consolata handed me a train ticket back to Inverness, and said, 'There, you can go now.'

But where was I to go? By then I had no other family that I knew of. I had no guidance, and no sense of how to live outside the walls of an institution. I had absolutely no idea what I was going to do next, and it broke my heart to leave Laura behind.

A few hours later I was on the train from Edinburgh to Inverness, and I still hadn't a clue where I was going to go when I got there.

So I decided I should look for my dad. I could hardly remember him at all – I hadn't seen him since that time he took us out of the orphanage and got drunk in the restaurant. I barely knew the person I was looking for, and couldn't have described him, but I knew what area of Inverness to go to, because when I saw Jason at the boys' home he'd told me Dad still lived there.

So I was off the train, wandering around Inverness, asking questions to see if anyone knew him, or knew of him. Eventually I was in a shop and a man overheard me and said, 'I know your dad. I'm staying with him and his girlfriend. Come with me, and I'll take you to his house.' And he took me to my dad's house near the ferry port, a stone's throw from where we lived as a family when I was a toddler.

The man who'd taken me there knocked on the door, and my dad answered. I don't know what I'd been expecting, but he didn't look good: a small, greasy-looking guy, bald and shifty. From the moment I set eyes on him, I knew I didn't trust him. But what could I do?

'This girl was in the shop, she's looking for her father. I asked her what her father's name was and she says it's you,' said the man who'd brought me there.

'You're my dad,' I said to the guy behind the door.

'What are you doing here?' he asked me.

'I'm looking for you. I've come from Edinburgh. I have nowhere to go, no place. I need somewhere to stay.'

He said, 'Well, you can't stay here with me.'

'But you're my father; I've got nowhere to go.'

'Ok,' he said, reluctantly. 'You can stay here. But only for a few days.'

And true to his word, my dad threw me out after a couple of days.

~~~

~13~

After that I was homeless and, for the first time in my life, I was on my own in the world. I slept rough a lot, outside on the streets. I was very cold, and completely alone. It's hard for me to write about this time in my life: I was desperately unwell, mentally and physically, and tried to kill myself three times with overdoses. These were serious suicide attempts – I had absolutely no intention of carrying on living – but somehow each time I was found and taken to hospital to have my stomach pumped. On the third time, I overheard a doctor saying, 'It's a fifty-fifty chance here, we don't think she's going to make it.' The desire to end my life – to end my own suffering in the only way I could –

stayed with me for many years. I still find it almost too painful to think of that poor wee girl, not even sixteen, out on the streets, just wanting to die.

Soon after those suicide attempts I met some people who introduced me to alcohol, though I didn't like it much. One of them, David, was living in a caravan at the time, and he drank a lot. I stayed in a few different places with these people, once in David's caravan. I'd stopped trying to kill myself by this time, but I was self-harming a lot, cutting my arms and legs with razors. I just felt dirty and ashamed all the time.

This David started asking me to meet him on my own, and the first couple of times I didn't go because I was afraid. But then, when we did start going out, he was the perfect gentleman. He'd buy me juice and chocolates and show me affection, and I thought 'wow, somebody loves me, somebody really wants me'. Of course, I had no idea what love was – I'd never experienced it. So I thought that was love.

Looking back at my sixteen-year-old self, I can see that inside I was still just the same scared, abused little girl who had first gone into the orphanage. A child who was afraid of everything and just wanted her mum and dad. All I ever wanted was to be loved, to have a place to live, to belong to someone. And soon – sadly – I belonged to David.

He was ten and a half years older than me – so twenty-seven to my sixteen when we met. When I first used to go to the caravan he'd want me to sleep with him, but I wouldn't. I went to bed with all my clothes on, shoes on and everything. I was still a virgin. He'd try to give me alcohol, but I'd only take little sips because I didn't like the way it made me feel. Eventually he just took my clothes off without asking, and did what he wanted.

After that, I lived with David in the caravan, and to begin with it was OK. But I really knew nothing. I had no idea how to cook – I couldn't make a single meal – or how to shop or keep house.

The first time he told me to go to the shop to get the groceries, I couldn't think what to shop for. I put it off, telling him I'd go in a minute, in a minute . . . then, when I finally ran out of excuses, I went to the shop, but I was so confused I came back empty-handed.

'Where are the groceries?'

'I didn't know what to get.'

When I said that, he punched me in the mouth so hard I bit through my lip. I've still got the scar.

And that's when he began beating me. He beat me because I had no mother, no father, nobody to show me how to be. And because I'd had no guidance, I didn't even know enough to say it was wrong. When you've had no love in your life from your parents, you're always looking for somebody to love you. You look for security that way. It's the same for so many women who've come out of care. If anything, the beatings were just a familiar scenario – from Ada Stevenson, from the nuns.

I had black eyes constantly; I wore sunglasses winter and summer. He'd rape me whenever he felt like it, and beat me for no apparent reason. But by this time, I just felt I'd been a victim all my life, and I couldn't see any way out of it.

Sometimes, when I tell my story to people who haven't been through domestic abuse, they ask 'Why didn't you just leave?' Maybe you're thinking that, too, if you haven't experienced extreme violence and coercive control. But – as I was to find out on numerous occasions in the years to come – it's just not that easy.

At the end of the second year, I fell pregnant with my first son, and we moved out of the caravan into a house.

~ ~ ~

~14~

David was an alcoholic; he drank like a fish. We lived together, but he ran around with a lot of other women. He used to call me his trophy, because I was so young and innocent.

The beatings and sexual violence continued. I tried to leave him countless times, but I knew no other way of life. He'd tell me this was normal, that this was how people lived – and because I'd never had anything in my life to compare it to, I'd believe him and come back. And it would all happen all over again.

It was such a repeating pattern during these years, it's hard to separate out individual incidents; they just all blur together. But I remember the time he shattered my arm. I was cleaning the windows and I must have done something he didn't like – who knows what, it could have been anything – and he took the broom and battered my right arm. He broke it in three places, then refused to take me to hospital. Somehow I got to hospital – I think a neighbour must have taken me.

The doctor said, 'How did that happen?'

'I climbed a tree,' I said, 'and I fell.'

Of course, the doctor didn't believe a word of this. 'You didn't fall out of a tree,' he said. 'Someone did this to you, didn't they.' But I was too afraid to say.

My arm was in plaster for six weeks and David did show me a little sympathy during that time, but as soon as the plaster came off he started again.

Here's another typical scene:

David comes home and asks where his dinner is.

'It's in the oven,' I say.

'Well, can I have it?'

'It's not ready yet.'

'What have you been doing all day anyway?'

'I've been cleaning.' (That's what I did, all day every day.)

'Doesn't look clean to me.'

'Well, I have.'

And a little retort like that would be all it took. I had lovely long hair at that time and he used to grab me by the hair and pull me around the floor, kicking and punching me. One time he pulled me all the way out of the door by my hair and along the pathway, and my knees got so much gravel in them I couldn't walk.

I hadn't been ready to have kids. I was still a child myself. I did my best, but because of my attempts to leave David the authorities knew about my situation as an unmarried mother, and when I was eighteen the social services took my first two sons and forced me to give them up for adoption. It was brutal, the way I was treated by the system at that time – I was judged and punished when I should have been understood and helped – and afterwards, I was like a zombie. I didn't feel I was alive at all; I was hollow, just going through the motions.

The doctor put me on contraception and told me to hide the pills from David, but it was too difficult to get out of the house to collect the prescriptions on time without him knowing what I was doing, and over the next decade I had another six children.

~ ~ ~

~15~

One day, when David was away, his brother came to visit the house. When David came home, I said, 'Your brother was here looking for you today.'

'How long did he stay?'

'Not long, I made him a cup of coffee.'

And that was all it took to convince David that I was now sleeping with his brother. He kept asking, 'What did you do with him? What did you do?' until eventually I went to bed.

When he came to bed he was still going on about it, insisting I'd had sex with his brother.

Eventually, I said, 'Well, if that's what you want to believe, you believe it.'

At that, he jumped out of bed, took the poker from the fire, and started beating me on the legs. My legs were coming up in big lumps, and he started on my arms, my tummy, all over my body. David's beatings were usually short and sharp, but this time he just wasn't stopping. By now I had a little girl, Marie – she was just a baby, six months old at the most. This beating went on through the night, while my baby was asleep in her cot. Incredibly, Marie slept through it all.

He beat me for hours. I remember begging him to just kill me, because I couldn't stand it anymore. Eventually he tired and fell asleep. I was in agony, I could barely move, but I knew how close he'd been to killing me, and I knew I had to get out of there before he woke up. Somehow I was able to drag my clothes on – and to this day, I have no idea how I managed it. Only God could have given me the strength to get up off that bed. Just as I was putting on my shoes, he moved. In a blind panic I pulled myself out of the back door, leaving Marie behind.

I made it to the nearby police station and told the officer there that I'd been beaten badly.

'You don't look beaten to me,' she said. But she took me into a room with another female officer, and I stripped down, and when they saw what he'd done to me they were shocked. 'Whoever did this was an animal,' the second officer said. I told her it was David, and she said, 'You know we have no choice – we have an obligation now to go and arrest this man. Are you OK with that?' I said I was, and explained that I'd left my daughter there. They left me safely in the police station, and went to arrest David.

But when they came back they didn't have Marie. David must have realised when he woke up that I'd gone to the police, and he'd got one of his brothers to take my baby girl and hide her, as a hostage, so that I wouldn't press charges. But the police reassured me that they'd find my daughter and get us to a place of safety, and that's what they did. David was arrested and taken to prison on a serious charge – an indictment of attempted murder.

And that should have been the end of the story of my relationship with David. But I was still young, and silly, and his brother met with me and told me how David was suffering in prison, and how long he'd be incarcerated for if he was found guilty, and he and begged me to go and visit him. I refused at first, but then gave in. I saw him in the prison, and he said he was sorry for what he'd done to me.

'Sorry?' I said. 'No amount of sorry is going to take away all the pain I've suffered at your hands. You nearly killed me.'

'Elaine,' he said, 'I promise I'll make it up to you. Please don't do this to me. Get me out of here and I'll prove to you I can be everything you want me to be.'

And I fell for that, because, as I say, I was foolish and naive. So I went to the Procurator Fiscal (the public prosecutor in Scotland) and said I wanted to drop the charges.

David got out, and everything was fine for two weeks, then it started again. Exactly the same as before.

There were times in those years when I was so desperate I'd plan to poison him. I'd put bleach in his food and make up all sorts of mixtures that could kill him, because I didn't see any other way out for me. But I never gave them to him. I couldn't bring myself to do it.

Instead, I started self-harming again. I took razors into the bath and cut myself all over my arms and legs. I felt so sick and desperate. I still have those scars. And I know, now, how common this is, when you feel there's no way out; when there's nowhere for the feelings of pain and desperation to go. In later years, I've met many women who have been raped routinely by their husbands, and who would cut themselves afterwards.

~~~

~16~

The beatings were bad, and the verbal abuse was worse. David never missed an opportunity to tell me that I was fat, ugly, worthless and stupid, and that I'd never amount to anything – and I believed it.

But looking back, the control he had over me was the worst thing of all, and that was constant. David controlled everything. He controlled when I watched TV, and what I watched, what I ate, what I wore, what time I went to bed, when I got up. He controlled who I saw – when people came to the house to visit, he'd say to me, 'Go into the bedroom.' And I'd go.

He'd lock doors on me, and lock me in the house whenever he went out during the day. The house we lived in was isolated, in bleak countryside in Morayshire, way up in the north-east of Scotland. It was four miles from any town, which is a long walk with small children, and of course, I couldn't drive a car. Every week I'd ask him, 'Is it OK if I go out today and take the kids for a walk into the town?'

'You don't need to go out,' he'd say.

So we never went out.

When he did let me out to do the shopping, he'd go through all the bags, check the receipt, count the change, everything. The kids and I loved cornflakes, but when I came home one day with boxes of cornflakes, he said, 'Who told you to buy cornflakes?'

'Nobody,' I said, 'but the kids need breakfast.'

He took the boxes of cornflakes and threw them in the bin. The food he wanted to eat was worse than orphanage food – mince and potatoes, every day. Anything else I tried to buy the kids – any kind of treat at all – went straight in the bin.

I was never allowed to wear make-up, or clothes that I chose. I loved wearing white, but if I put anything white on, he'd tell me to take it off. When he gave me money to buy clothes I'd go to the supermarket and buy the kinds of things I liked, but he'd always insist on inspecting the bags when I got back.

'Let me see what you've bought,' he'd say, and I'd show him.

'No, you can't wear that. Take it back to the shop; you're not allowed to wear that.'

One day as he was leaving the house, he said he wouldn't be back till late that night, so I decided I was going to put on some make-up and dress up nicely in some of my old clothes, just to see what it looked like. It was lovely! I felt a sense of lightness and possibility, like I was a real person again. I kept the clothes and make-up on, thinking that maybe when David saw me like that, he'd feel differently. But he just slapped me hard in the face and said, 'Get that off, only whores wear stuff like that.'

So the only clothes I had were the clothes he wanted me to wear. Long skirts. Big tops. Scratchy, woollen things – like the clothes the nuns made us wear. I have a couple of photos of myself around that age, and when I look at them now, I see a pretty young woman with a lovely figure. But I hardly knew it at the time – I was banned from taking any pleasure in clothes or any care over my appearance, and he treated our daughters the same way.

From the very beginning, he'd told me that the way were living was normal; that this is how everyone behaved. But he was brainwashing me, and he knew it. He knew I had no one to turn to for a different perspective. And I was used to being told what to do by the nuns, and used to being punished if I didn't do what I was told – he knew that too.

All this time, I was getting pregnant and having babies. After my first two sons had been taken away, I didn't want any more children, but he kept telling me that another child would make things better between us. In recent years I've heard many other survivors of domestic abuse say that they were told the same, but of course it's not true. The rapes and pregnancies were just another form of control. He was trapping me all the time with more children.

~~~

~17~

Looking back, it's clear to me that David had been badly warped by his own upbringing, and was seriously mentally ill, though he masked it very well at the beginning. The amount he drank would have twisted his mind even more over the years, too.

David's father had been unbelievably strict. They weren't even allowed Christmas when he was a kid, and he tried to ban Christmas in our house too. Around the middle of December every year I'd say, 'I'll put the tree up,' and he'd say, 'No tree in this house, no Christmas here. My father never allowed Christmas so why should I.'

Eventually he gave in, because the kids were so upset by the idea of Santa not being able to come, but he never liked it.

He hit the kids too, and they were constantly afraid of putting a foot wrong. When he was in the house they spent all their time in their bedrooms. There was never any family time, playing games or watching TV, and everything always had to be in its rightful place. Sometimes he'd go out for a few hours and I'd jump on the beds with the kids and have pillow fights, but we'd always have to make sure everything was spotless by the time he walked through the door. The one time he came back early and caught us all playing, he made the kids throw everything they'd been playing with into the bin. He was a control freak, and cruel and crazy with it.

We never had any money in the early years. But suddenly, after a decade or so, David stopped drinking all the time and started earning money, and before long he was a pretty rich man. He also stopped beating me. All of which you'd think would be good news – except that as the beatings stopped the verbal abuse escalated, and in so many ways, that was worse. I've heard a lot of women say that when they hit you it's bad, but when they abuse you with words, it touches something deeper inside you. And he wasn't earning all this money at a job. He'd become a drug dealer.

He never really told me anything about what he did, but I knew he was taking drugs and I knew that all the cars and fancy stuff in the house and all the money rolling in must have come from somewhere. It didn't take much to work it out.

Then there was a police raid. They came to the house while the children were there, and they found drugs in the house. I was shattered: I thought I'd been doing everything I could to bring the kids up well and protect them from David, and all the time he'd been keeping drugs in the home. I don't know exactly what it was they found, but somehow David got off without a prison sentence.

Not long after, when the kids were at school, I was cleaning the house and found some little tablets around the sofa – little chunky tablets with letters printed on them. I was still very sheltered and naive at this time, but even I could work out what these were. And I knew that if one of the kids had got hold of them and thought they were sweeties, David would be in prison for the rest of his days.

I bided my time, and then later on that night, I showed one of the tablets to him and said, 'What's this?'

'Where did you find that?'

'It was on the floor; there were two or three of them. What the heck are you into? What are you doing? This is drugs isn't it.'

'Oh no,' he said. 'That's just a headache pill.'

But I wasn't that stupid, and it was clear he was on something as his behaviour became more and more erratic – he'd have violent fits, throwing things around, smashing up the house, threatening to kill us all. He was obviously taking the ecstasy he dealt. And there was another drug too, which I only knew about because he tricked me into rubbing it on my gums when I had a toothache. I'd asked him to go out for painkillers, but this was his solution. Suddenly my head was pounding, and my limbs went floppy – then I couldn't feel my body at all, my eyes stopped working, and I fell to the ground. I was terrified, and begged him to take me to hospital, but he just told me to walk around outside and drink a lot of water. The effects went on for days – I couldn't sleep at all, and thought I was going crazy. He'd given me a massive dose of an amphetamine, speed, and it could easily have killed me. But he knew I wouldn't go to the police. That's the level of control he had over me.

~~~

Part Four

Hagar was a single mother
She was abandoned by the family she belonged to
And there in the wilderness with her son alone
With very little provision
She was wondering
She was questioning
Does anyone care?

She's crying in the desert
She's lost in her despair
She thinks nobody loves her
Hagar thinks nobody's there
But God says

I will be a ring of fire around her
And I will be the glory in her midst
And the power of my presence
Will bring her to her knees
And I will lift her up again

For I'm the God who sees

I'm the God who sees

Then He speaks in gentle whispers

And He softly calls her name

She feels His arms enfold her

As He holds her

And she'll never be the same . . .

From 'The God Who Sees', lyrics by Nicole
C. Mullen and Kathie Lee Gifford

~18~

I could have died so many times, whether from neglect, despair, violence or abuse. Whenever I wonder at the fact that I survived my early childhood and everything which followed, and am still alive to tell you this story today, I think of that beautiful song, 'The God Who Sees'.

The song begins with the story of Hagar (Genesis, chapters 16 and 21). Hagar was a slave who gave birth to Abraham's son Ishmael, but was then driven out into the desert by Abraham's jealous wife Sarah. Hagar was treated with incredible cruelty, but her story is one of hope. As she and Ishmael were close to death in the desert, having run out of food and water, she cried to God. Although she was an outcast, a nobody, a victim of abandonment and abuse, God rescued Hagar. He saw her pain and distress and sent her comfort, showing her how to find water so she could survive her ordeal, and promising her hope for the future.

I also think often of Shadrach, Mesach and Abednego in the Old Testament (Daniel 3: 16–28) who were bound and thrown into the fiery furnace by King Nebuchadnezzar. But they didn't burn: when the King's men looked into the furnace they saw Shadrach, Mesach and Abednego walking around in the fire, with a fourth man, the Son of God, who was there in the furnace with them, and brought them safely out of the flames.

It was in 1992, when I'd been with David for over fifteen years, and just a couple of months after I'd given birth to my little boy Matthew, when I was approached by a lady who asked me, 'Are you converted yet?'

'Converted?' I said, 'I don't know what you mean.'

She said, 'You know, Jesus loves you. He wants to save you.'

I was angry at this. 'Don't tell me that Jesus loves me,' I said. 'Because if Jesus loved me, why would he allow me to go through everything I've been through? You don't know about the life I've had.'

'Oh, but He loves you,' she said.

By this point, I was furious. 'Nobody loves me!' I retorted. 'I've been a reject from the day I was born. My mother didn't want me, my father didn't want me. Nobody wanted me.'

'Oh no, Elaine,' she replied, 'You're very precious in the eyes of God.'

And she started telling me that God knows about the life I've had, and that He's been there in it with me, and that He was going to help me through it. At the time, I blocked it out. I just wasn't interested.

But later it kept going round in my mind. 'Hmmm, this Jesus loves me?' I thought. 'He wants to save me?' So I started going to church, and as I was hearing about the Lord and about being Born Again, the messages started to sink in a little bit. Jesus came into this world to save the lost, they said – and I was very, very lost. Being there in the church reminded me of good times at the orphanage, hearing about Jesus from Martin at the Children's Happy Hour, and I got the feeling I had as a child, when I felt drawn towards the Christmas lights in the orphanage.

So I kept going to church, and the message of salvation was really starting to reach me, deep inside. One Sunday a woman there gave me a tract – like a little flyer. When I got home I sat down and read the whole tract, front to back and top to bottom, and there was a prayer at the end. I went down on my knees, and I spoke to God for the first time. I said, 'You know, Lord, I don't know if I can say this and mean it and walk with you throughout my life, but I'm going to try.' And I prayed the prayer that was printed on the bottom of the tract. And as I prayed, repenting of my sin and asking the Lord to forgive me, He came into my heart through the Spirit, and I felt such a lightness; such incredible peace. Until then it was as though I'd carried the weight of the world on my shoulders, but as I kept praying, it all fell away, and I've walked with God from that day till now.

On October 8th, 1992, I was baptized. When I went down into that water all my sin was crucified, as Christ was crucified on the cross, and when I came back up out of the water all my sin was washed away and I was brand new. Born Again. That was the day I knew that God had brought about my salvation, and I gave my life fully to the Lord.

~~~

~19~

Jesus replied, 'Very truly I tell you, no one can see the kingdom of God unless they are born again.'

'How can someone be born when they are old?' Nicodemus asked. 'Surely they cannot enter a second time into their mother's womb to be born!'

Jesus answered, 'Very truly I tell you, no one can enter the kingdom of God unless they are born of water and the Spirit. Flesh gives birth to flesh, but the Spirit gives birth to spirit. You should not be surprised at my saying, "You must be born again".'

John 3:3–7John 3:3–7

I'd been saved but I didn't fully enjoy my salvation, because life at home continued exactly as it was before; just one difficulty after another. I could never see the hand of God at work in my life, and I used say, 'God, I've given my life over to you. Why am I still suffering all this abuse?' I felt like I'd done what God wanted. I'd accepted Him and I was walking the righteous walk, but being a Christian in a house with David, trying to bring up the children, trying to do the right thing – it was so hard. For a long time, I doubted my faith. I doubted if I even *was* a Christian. But when I started using my Bible, trying to see what it was telling me, I started to see the good of God. And I could believe that although I was in the fiery furnace, He was with me, though I couldn't see Him.

As a young Christian trying to bring up a family, reading the Bible was like clinging to this God of mine, asking him to help me and strengthen me. And there were times when I was weak; times when I thought 'I just can't do this.' But I started learning, through the Bible, that God wants us to just take one day at a time. So I began to live like that, one day at a time, through the turmoil of it all. And each time I got through a day I'd thank God and say, 'Lord, you got me through this day, and that's a good thing.' I just went on like that for a long, long time, amid the verbal abuse and threats, and David smashing the house up whenever something didn't suit him. One day at a time, one day at a time. But it was a struggle.

To begin with, David didn't mind me going to church – he was running around with another woman at the time, and me being out of the house on a Sunday gave him more opportunity to see her. And for a while, he didn't mind me reading my Bible. But when he saw how often I was reading it, he started to object, and then started trying to ban the Bible completely. 'No Bible will be read in this house,' he would say to me, 'No Bibles allowed in this house. You will not open a Bible in this house.' So I thought, there's one way I can get to read my Bible – I'll go and have a bath. And I'd stick the Bible up my jumper or wrap it in a towel, and

I'd spend ages in the bathroom with the door locked, reading and reading. I had a lot of baths! And I started to see, through those pages, how much God loved me and what he'd done for me. Yet still I'd say, 'But God, you tell me you love me. Your son died on the cross for me. So why are you allowing me to suffer like this?' But I wasn't getting any answers.

We often wonder why God is allowing all the bad stuff to happen in our life. But the Bible was speaking to me, telling me that what the dark side meant for bad, God would turn around for good, as in the story of Joseph. Joseph's story was *my* story, though I couldn't see it yet.

Through all this, I prayed day and night, and I felt that God was protecting me. Every time David would say vicious, abusive things to me, or throw things around in the house, I'd run to the garden, go down on my knees and cry out to God – 'God, you have to help me. I don't know what to do.' I just couldn't see any way out for myself, though I knew that God was keeping me strong, and I had faith that one day He would set me free.

But as the years went on, nothing changed. I went to Church, read my Bible as often as I could, prayed to God day and night, but still I was trapped with David; with the verbal abuse and the control and the death threats, and his destructive violence in the house. I'd ask myself, 'Why am I not getting free of this? Why am I still living in this hell?'

I made a lot of lovely Christian friends at the church, who would listen to my story, and who saw my growing passion for Christ. They would pray for me, and I could feel those prayers strengthening me. I felt their love for me, that they were caring for me, and I knew they were praying to God to release me so I could live a better life. But even so, I was still stuck.

~~~

~20~

I nearly got away from David so many times, and every time I was forced to go back. I had six children still at home, some of them very young, and I couldn't go unless I took them with me. But they were scared of their dad, and it was impossible to get them all to agree to come away. If I had managed to get my kids all together it would have been different, but he'd brainwashed and threatened them so much that they were completely under his control. And by now David was a big drug dealer with contacts everywhere, so every time I left he'd make calls and put people out looking for me, and they always brought me back. It was just like the police bringing me back whenever I tried to escape from the convent as a young teenager back in Edinburgh. Then he'd torment me, telling me I was a bad mother, and that if I didn't stop running away he'd report me to the Social Services. And that was the clincher: those children were my life, and the thought of having them taken away was just too much. I couldn't bear it.

The police knew that David was abusing me, and the local authority, Elgin Council, knew that I was trying to leave, because I went to them on numerous occasions, telling them everything I'd been through and asking for emergency accommodation. But every time, I ended up back with David. The homeless officer, Richard, said to me 'Elaine, you're just not ready to take this step yet. But we'll be here for you when you are.'

Through all of this, my Christian friends showed me nothing but compassion. They just kept praying for me and supporting me. Through these friends, I was beginning to see the kind of life I could live: a simple life of faith, spreading the word of God's love. I didn't want money or possessions, I just wanted this one thing, to be free to walk with God. That was my dream of happiness: to have my freedom.

Then David stopped running around with other women and decided to put a stop to my churchgoing. His controlling behaviour was escalating again. On the rare Sundays he let me go, he'd give me a deadline to be back. I'd prepare food on a Saturday night for the next day so I could get going to church in the morning. The service itself was only about an hour long, but afterwards we'd have coffee, share the Bible and talk about how our week had been. One Sunday there had been a lot of conversation; I'd been getting strength and support from talking with the people who were there, and I was back late.

'What time do you call this?' he said.

I said, 'I'm sorry, I couldn't get back any earlier. People talk, it takes time, it can't be helped.'

He picked up the TV and threw it at me. 'You've got kids to feed,' he said, and then started ranting on about how the Pastor was probably chatting me up. All at once, the strength and optimism I'd gained from Church drained away, and I felt worthless once again.

I cried, 'No – that's not the way of it. I go to church for Jesus because I love Him, and I want to learn.'

He told me I wasn't going to church any more, because I couldn't get back in time, and said he was going to go and see the Pastor himself and tell him that. I thought, 'Why don't you go and tell the Pastor what you're doing to me,' but I didn't say anything, of course.

~ ~ ~

~21~

The Lord is near to the brokenhearted

and saves the crushed in spirit.

Psalm 34:18

In around 2002, I started watching Christian TV, and particularly a lady called Joyce Meyer, an American evangelist. Whenever David was out, I'd watch her, and if I heard him coming in I'd switch the TV off immediately, because he didn't like me watching TV of any kind.

I was especially interested in Joyce Meyer's broadcasts because she was a victim herself of abuse, from her father and also her first husband. One day I was watching, and she said, 'If any of you ladies are in a relationship and these things are happening – you need to get out. Because these people – the abusers, the perpetrators, they try to tell you that this is normal, they brainwash you, they control everything.' And – oh, gosh, the shock of it – suddenly, I realised that she knew the truth of my life, and that my experiences were shared by others, too. And I knew, once and for all, that the next time God made an escape for me, I'd have to take it, no matter what.

After a while, David would watch TV with me too, but he'd always turn Joyce Meyer off – I think because he felt convicted when she talked about men who abuse women, and about how angry God is with abusers. I'd thought that maybe now I was a Christian he would change. I saw in the Bible all the places where God abhors violence against women, and I prayed and prayed that He would grab David and turn him around, but it wasn't happening.

I started writing letters to Joyce Meyer, telling her all about what had happened in my life, and I'd get letters back – not from her personally, but from people who worked in her ministry and knew her heart. They'd say, 'We're praying for you, and one day God will set you free from all this, just as He set Joyce free.'

I could see the happy life that Joyce Meyer had, and deep in my heart, I could feel that God had a plan for me. My parents may have rejected me, but I was beginning to experience God's love as that of my true father, protecting me and keeping me safe, for a purpose only He knew. I thought often of the Old Testament story of the orphan Esther, who became queen to King Xerxes, and whose courage saved the lives of all the Jews in Persia. When Mordecai learned of the plot to kill the Jews, he challenged Esther, saying, 'Who knows but that you have come to your royal position for such a time as this?' (Esther 4:14). The phrase 'for such a time as this' echoed round in my mind, chiming with the feeling that when I finally got free, God would show me the way to help others.

I remember taking my Bible and writing in it, 'Jesus, one day I'll get out of here, and then I'll do something great for you.'

But little did I know what I'd have to go through before I could finally grasp my freedom. The flames of the fiery furnace were about to get bigger.

~ ~ ~

Part Five

Even though I walk

through the valley of the shadow of death

I will fear no evil,

for you are with me;

your rod and your staff,

they comfort me.

Psalm 23:4

~22~

In 2012 I noticed I was losing weight, but I didn't think much about it. Then, when I went to the toilet, I started seeing blood in my poo. I assumed it was constipation, but it was getting worse, and I had a growing pain in my side, so I told my daughter Louise. At that time, Louise was sixteen, and we were very close. She told me I had to go to the doctor, but I was afraid of the tests they'd do. I was always a such a fearful person, but now I was terrified. Not of illness, I wasn't even thinking about that, but of having my private parts examined. I was full of shame, because David used to force himself on me from the back and anally rape me, and there was a lot of pain and trauma there.

Eventually, Louise persuaded me to go to the doctor, and the doctor sent me to a consultant at the hospital – Mr Das, an Indian man. I explained what was happening, and he described the tests he'd have to do, and somehow I plucked up the courage to tell him what my husband did to me, and told him I wouldn't be able to handle those tests. Mr Das was lovely; he promised they'd give me a general anaesthetic and put me to sleep for the tests.

Mr Das woke me up after the tests, and said I'd be staying in hospital for another day because of the amount of anaesthetic they'd given me. So I was in the ward at about eight o'clock that night when I heard his footsteps coming along the corridor.

'Hello,' he said, 'how are you feeling?'

'I'm fine, doctor.'

'Well, I don't come with good news. I'm afraid what I saw today doesn't look very good at all. I think you might have cancer.'

I just froze. 'God,' I thought, 'everything I've been through in my life and now this. I just can't take any more.'

I said to Mr Das, 'How can you tell me that if you're not sure? What do I tell my family? What do I do?' And his reaction felt cold and dismissive to me. He said, 'You'll deal with it.'

I remember weeping and crying to Mr Das, 'I don't want to die! I've got a life! I value my life!'

I'd tried so hard to kill myself in the past, and had suffered decades of constant abuse since, but at that moment I knew, more than anything, that I wanted to live. I prayed to God to soften that doctor's heart, and He did: in the months afterwards, Mr Das became my best friend.

I stayed in hospital until the test results came back, and it was rectal cancer. I was terrified, convinced I was going to die. Everyone back at the church prayed and prayed – I was saturated in prayer and I could feel their love flowing towards me.

The Pastor said, 'This is not the end of your story, Elaine. God has more in store for you.'

I said, 'More? Surely not more of this!'

'No,' he said, 'your story's going to have a good ending.'

Despite all the love and prayer, I felt like I was inside a bottle with a cork on it. I couldn't speak to my kids. I wouldn't speak to anyone, because I was so sure I was going to die. My thoughts were so dark – I kept thinking 'I've been a victim all my life, though I've never hurt anybody. I've never done anything bad to anyone, yet no one in my life has ever loved me or wanted me.' I was spiralling down.

Then Sally, one of my Christian friends, came to see me. 'Elaine,' she said, 'you're not going to die. God has a plan for your life. You need to trust in Him.'

I remembered Psalm 139 – 'all the days ordained for me were written in your book' – and then I just hung on to God, drawing strength from Him. All the time I was ill I told others about God and how God can give us hope.

The initial treatment was five weeks: radiotherapy and chemo, and I had to go to Aberdeen, seventy-five miles away, for that. The tumour was big: three centimetres. I was so scared – I had no idea what was going on, how it was going to be, and whether I'd survive. But I was also full of God's love. When I walked into that cancer ward and saw all the other people sitting there, women with no hair, my heart bled for them.

I was taken over to my seat and hooked up to the drip. There was another lady there, Erica, with her husband, and they asked me if it was my first time. Her husband said, 'You're only a young woman. You'll make it. You're going to be fine.' And I took such strength from that. I told them I was a Christian and Erica asked me to pray for her – she'd had cancer for a long time, and it kept coming back. I met so many nice folk in the cancer ward, and I'd tell them a bit about my life; share the story of where I'd been and what I'd gone through. And I'd just reach out to them. My heart was softening, and I felt for those women. And they'd ask me, 'Elaine, would you pray for me?' and I did – I prayed for everyone on that cancer ward. I took in books and tracts, trying to reach out to as many folk as I could, telling them about the better life God has in store for us – not on this earth, but in the heavenly realm.

One time my little sister Laura came to visit me at the hospital. Ever since I'd first met David he'd tried his best to keep people away from me, but he had to go to the toilet, so she came to sit with me, and she was able to hug me. She put a bracelet on me and an identical one on her own wrist, and said that meant we were walking in this together. She said, 'Are you afraid, Elaine?'

I said, 'I'm so afraid. But I'll tell you this, Laura, if I make it through this, I'm finally leaving him.'

~ ~ ~

~23~

From my little church, the prayers for me went worldwide. I found it really difficult to think of so many people around the world reaching out for me and praying for me. How was it happening? How did I deserve it? People I didn't even know were getting in touch with me, telling me that good will come of my life, that God has blessings for me that will overflow; that I won't even be able to hold. I was getting messages saying 'God's going to come through for you,' and 'God's going to bring you out of the oppression you're under.'

That five weeks of treatment was gruelling – by the end I could hardly sit because of the pain. But I'd tell the nurses that I believed God was going to heal me. And then, just at the last two weeks of treatment, I felt something happen in my body. I just felt it. My bloods seemed to stay the same, the cancer didn't move, but I just knew it – I knew I was healed. And I said to the nurses, 'I'm going to get through this. My faith will take me through.' I'd been afraid of losing my hair – I had lovely long, straight hair, and I kept pulling on it to see if it was coming out. But it didn't – instead, it went curly, which was even nicer!

After my last radiotherapy day I was allowed to go home for a month to recover, and that month was terrible. David was still yelling and bawling all the time, and I wasn't getting any of the basic peace and rest I needed to recover. The radiotherapy had damaged my rectum and bowel so much that I couldn't poo – I was screaming in pain. I remember one day I felt so weak, I fell to the floor. I thought I was going to die right there, and I prayed to God 'Lord, help me, please – but if you want to take me, please just take me now so I can be free of all this.'

At the end of that month, Mr Das called me at home.

'Hello, Elaine, how are you?'

'Don't ask me how I am, Doctor, I'm suffering terribly! I'm in such pain.'

He said, 'You come and see me tomorrow.'

'I can't come tomorrow,' I said, 'I'm going to church.'

'Oh, you're going to church?'

'Yes, I am, I have to.'

'Well then, you come and see me on Monday.'

So I went to church the next day, and all my friends were so happy to see me. When I walked through the door, they said, 'Elaine, you look so well! You're glowing! And your hair's curly!'

And it was true – despite all the pain, I *was* glowing.

Then on the Monday I went to see Mr Das, and he said the same. He said they would still have to operate to get rid of the tumour, and he sent me for scans – but then, they couldn't find the tumour. After I'd had the scans a second time, Mr Das took me into his office, laid his papers on the table and said, 'Here, look at this. We can't find the tumour. We don't even know *where* to operate now.'

It had gone! At that moment, I knew for sure that I really was healed. I said to Mr Das 'I believe God has healed me, through your hands and the hands of the other doctors.'

But Mr Das said they still needed to operate to make sure there was nothing left. A date was set, for November 7th, 2012. Seven is my favourite number, and in the Bible, seven is the sign of completion, so it was an auspicious date – but I was still convinced the surgery wouldn't be necessary.

I went to my church and said, 'Pastor, what do I do? I know I'm healed: do I let them operate, or do I walk in faith?'

It would be a huge, risky operation. Because they couldn't actually *see* the tumour, they'd have to cut me from groin to chest, and I didn't want to go through it if there was no need.

But the Pastor said, 'Elaine, if it was me I'd let them operate, just to make sure there isn't anything lurking.'

I was in the operating theatre for six or seven hours. After the operation I was in intensive care for forty-eight hours, hooked up to all sorts of machines, with tubes in me.

My surgeon had gone away for the weekend, but there were five other surgeons looking after me, and when I woke up in intensive care, they all came round, one by one, and told me the operation had been a success. I was still in terrible pain, and sedated with morphine and so weak I couldn't even speak, but I remember that when I woke up my Pastor was there, praying for me, two of my children were there, and so was their father.

By the Monday I was back on the cancer ward, and Mr Das came to see me. I still felt very weak and sick, but he encouraged me to try and eat a little, and as the days went by I started to get stronger.

My family visited every day, and I remember my son Matthew saying to me, 'You know, no woman should have to go through what you've been through. You're strong, Mum.' My children were beginning to see how hard my life had been, how much their father had hurt me, and how my faith had got me through the cancer. For the first time, I felt that my children might be able to understand things from my perspective.

After ten days, Mr Das came to tell me I could go home – but he also said that if I didn't feel I was ready to go, I could stay. I think he knew that if I went home I wouldn't get the care I needed. In fact I didn't want to go home at all, because I knew what I'd be going back to.

The truth is that when I was in the hospital, I was safe. It was like going back to the orphanage in a strange way, because as an adult, I'd never known what it was like to just go to bed and sleep without fear. With David I was always on the alert for what he was going to do next, because even after the beatings stopped, he tortured me terribly with his words, and his rages were fierce. I'd often go to bed fully dressed because I never knew what was going to happen in the night, and more than once I ran for my life into the fields behind the house and slept there, even in the pouring rain, because I was so afraid of him.

But I had to go home, and David came to pick me up. 'Don't worry,' he said, 'I'll look after you. I'll do everything for you'.

The next morning he gave me breakfast in bed, but the morning after that it was business as usual, screaming and bawling again. 'I can't do this! I can't do this!' he was shouting. As ever, he just wanted all the attention, and couldn't stand for me to be getting any care. My daughter Louise said, 'What can't you do? My mum nearly died and all you can say is 'I can't do this, I can't do that'. It's your place to take care of her.' But in the end it was Louise who looked after me.

~~~

~24~

By late November it was cold and snowing, and I was still resting in bed. I'd got an infection and the doctor had been out to treat me with antibiotics. He'd said I might have to go back into hospital, but I'd started recovering again. I was still very weak though, and in constant pain, and I was upset that I wouldn't be able to do Christmas for the kids, even though they said, 'We don't care about Christmas, as long as we've got you, and you get well.'

People were sending beautiful bouquets to the house, and cards and gifts, and all of it angered David. 'No more of all this coming to the house,' he said. It was mad – I'd nearly died, and he was jealous of the attention I was getting.

By now I was a much stronger Christian, and I knew that the time was coming for me to finally leave. Just as I knew that God had healed me through the hands of the doctors, I knew the time was close when I'd be getting free of this situation. My faith was strong; I just had to get strong enough in my body.

On one of those days, during the hard snow at the end of 2012, David came into the bedroom and said, 'You know what, Elaine? You need to get up out of that bed and you need to walk. You need to go and walk three times around the yard because lying in bed all day and is not doing your muscles or your bones any good.' Well, obviously I was lying in bed all day because I was recovering from a major operation and a post-operation infection, and because staying in bed is what the doctors had *instructed* me to do – and apart from anything else, I could barely move. It was crazy, his reasoning was totally illogical. It was just control. But my old fear of him was still there, and all the brainwashing and conditioning of the past, and so I did it.

I was struggling on the floor, trying to put my boots on, when Louise came in.

'What are you doing?' she said.

'I'm going outside to the garden'

'What are you going out there for?'

'Because your father says I have to get up and walk three times around the garden otherwise my bones will get weak and my muscles will seize up.'

Louise said, 'He's mad.'

Then David came up and said 'Get up. I told you to get up and start walking,' and Louise lost her temper with him.

'Do you want to kill her?' she said, 'Is that your plan? If anything happens to her, it'll be on your shoulders!'

But he insisted, so out I went and tried to walk round the garden. The temperature was below zero, the snow was thick and hard, the ground was slippery, and that yard was big. A few times I thought I was going to collapse. And while I was staggering about, bent double with the effort, my eldest daughter Marie phoned my mobile.

'How are you doing, Mum?'

'Oh, I'm OK.'

'Well, you don't sound OK, Mum. What are you doing?'

'I'm outside in the yard.'

'What are you doing out in the yard?'

'Your father said I have to get up and walk around the yard because if I don't move I won't get better.'

'Mum, get back inside that house right away, and get into your bed. I'm going to phone and tell him.'

As I went back to the house I heard him on the phone to her, shouting and carrying on – it was just crazy.

As the weeks passed I started to get stronger again. I could get out of bed and go into the living room and have visitors. I was getting a lot of prayer, and my Pastor would come to the house to check I was OK. I could tell that when he came he was seeing things he didn't like. And I started to see David's controlling behaviour more clearly, noticing his anger whenever someone came to the house and told me I was looking well.

The Pastor came out to see me one day. He said, 'How are you Elaine?' and I think my face must have said it all. He knew; he could tell what it was like for me.

While I was ill David wouldn't cook, and the church organised for people to make meals and bring them to the house. It was wonderful, they made beautiful meals for us. But David was always complaining about the food, how he didn't like it, and didn't see why they were bringing it. I told him, 'This is what Christ does, through other people.' But he was just moaning and groaning about everything.

So as soon as I was fit enough I was up and cooking food and I remember saying to God one day in the kitchen, 'Lord, if you want me out of here, get me out. Because I can't live this way anymore. I'm ready to walk out of here. You need to show me; tell me what to do, because I can't take any more of this.'

That night I had a dream that I was in the hairdressers. I dreamed I was having my hair cut, and one side of my hair was down to my ankles, but on the other side it was short. The next morning I told Louise about the dream, and she said, 'What do you think the dream was saying to you?'

Now as a Christian, I believe God was showing me something in that dream. I believe it was a message that this had been going on long enough now. I felt He was saying that a change was coming. And I felt such a peace in my heart. So I said to God, 'Lord, I feel in my heart that this is what you're saying, but if you want me to get out of here now, then you need to help me. You need to make the path smooth, so I can walk out.' And I packed a little bag, just with the essentials: toiletries, underwear, a change of clothes.

Later that day, I was cooking food for the kids and David came in and started screaming that I was taking too long making the food. I said it would be ready soon, and I swore under my breath. I said I wished he would shut the f___ up. I hardly ever swore, but I was just so angry.

He asked me, 'What did you say?'

I told him I'd said nothing, but he'd heard me. He said, 'You swore at me, didn't you.' And he started screaming and bawling at me again, and finally, the moment came. I switched off the cooker and picked up my little bag.

'Yes, I did swear at you,' I said. 'And see that door? I'm walking out of that door today, and I'm never coming back.' Looking back, I still can't believe I found the strength.

'Oh, you are, are you?' he sneered. 'You might go, but you'll be glad to come back again. You're nothing without me.'

'I'm leaving,' I said. 'You have tormented me, you have tortured me, you have almost destroyed me. But you know what? From today, it's finished. When I leave this house, that's it. And I'll tell you one thing before I leave here. I forgive you for all that you've done to me. You owe me nothing, and I owe you nothing. Just get on with your life and let me get on with mine.'

And I did it. I walked out for good.

~~~

Part Six

I waited patiently for the Lord;

he turned to me and heard my cry.

He lifted me out of the slimy pit,

out of the mud and mire;

he set my feet on a rock

and gave me a firm place to stand.

He put a new song in my mouth,

a hymn of praise to our God.

Psalm 40:1–3

~25~

This wasn't the first time I'd knocked at the door of Moray Council in Elgin – on many of my previous attempts to leave David I'd got as far as the housing office. Richard, the homelessness officer and Fiona, the housing officer, knew me well by this time, and I knew they liked me. They knew about my whole life – the abuse, the orphanage and the convent, as well as what I went through with David – and they'd seen me going back to David time and again. But this time, when I walked in with my little bag of clothes, they could tell straight away that things were different.

Fiona said, 'Elaine, are you ready for this now?'

I said, 'I am.'

They immediately arranged homeless accommodation for me and my daughter Louise in a little harbour town on the Moray coast. It was such a huge step – I was finally away from David, and this time for good. But as soon as we moved in, I began to get ill – not with cancer, but with the after-effects of all the trauma. I just couldn't settle there, and I didn't like being so far from Dr Gray's hospital in Elgin, where I was still having regular check-ups to make sure the cancer wasn't coming back. So they brought me back to Elgin and gave me homeless accommodation there.

In Elgin, my life blossomed. I could go to church as much as I wanted; I could go to lunch and coffee with my friends. I felt like a human being – like I was somebody. It was an amazing feeling, just to be free of all that turmoil. Every day felt like a new beginning – like it really was the first day of the rest of my life.

I was spending a lot of time with my friend Sally, the one who had urged me to trust God when I was first diagnosed with cancer. She was a street pastor, and she could see my passion to reach out to others, so she encouraged me to become a street pastor too.

Street pastors go out into town centres on a Friday and Saturday night, from nine in the evening until four in the morning, and help people who are having a bad time. Usually folk who've had too much alcohol, who are upset or sick, and have lost the people they were with. We'd get them taxis home, give them water to drink and flipflops if they'd lost their shoes. As a street pastor I was also evangelizing on the streets, which I loved to do. I loved reaching out to people, telling them there was hope.

Becoming a street pastor involves fifty hours of training and for me, completing this training was a real achievement. The feeling of pride and confidence I got from that was something I'd never experienced before, and it was amazing.

So I was telling people about Jesus, and I was getting stronger and stronger all the time. I was making new Christian friends, going to what we call house groups and Bible meetings. I was also telling my story to people, getting invitations to talk with groups of women in the homeless accommodation about what I'd been through, and I made some really strong friendships there too.

While I was living in the homeless flats in Elgin, David used to come round, always in a brand-new car, park outside and pump the horn, trying to force me out. He harassed me, tormenting me with phone calls, demanding that I go back.

With me out of the family home, David's control over the kids escalated. He'd always bullied them and they were afraid of him, and now they tormented me too, punishing me for leaving him. I knew in my heart that it wasn't really my kids doing that – David had been poisoning their minds since they were little – but it still hurt.

Through the ups and downs of life in the homeless flats in Elgin, I kept focussing on the future. I knew the homeless accommodation was temporary, and I could see a day when I'd get the keys to my own house. That's what I was holding out for: a home of my own.

~ ~ ~

~26~

Six months after I first moved into Elgin, on a Saturday in 2013, I heard the letterbox and I knew in my heart that this was the day. I went into the hall and got the envelope, and there it was: a letter telling me there was a council house for me. My own house! Better still, it would be right across the road from where one of my friends from the homeless flats was now living. It couldn't have been better! I was so excited.

When I went into the council office to pick up the keys, Fiona the housing officer was sat with tears pouring from her eyes. 'Elaine,' she said, 'you've no idea how long I've waited to hand you these keys. You're free, Elaine. You'll never go back. I know that, and so do you.' And she hugged me. We were both crying.

Richard the homeless officer came out of his office and said, 'Anything you need, you just tell us.' The people at the council were just amazing. They furnished the flat for me, and came out to support me. I really felt like they thought I was someone worth helping. Like they believed in me.

And suddenly, I really was free. I was well, I was happy. I was living a useful and productive life with the church, achieving good things as a street pastor, reaching out to people. I had good friends, and I was meeting new folk all the time, telling my story and spreading the word of Jesus. I just loved my freedom. I was still deeply wounded inside but I knew I was healing. For the first time in my life, I felt truly valued – and, gradually, I started to value myself too.

Right from when I was sixteen and first with David, I could never look at myself in a mirror. I was full of shame; I felt so dirty and rejected, and I carried those feelings through every day of my life, for decades. As a woman, I could only think of myself as ugly and fat, because that's what he told me I was. Then one day at church I met a woman who had been through similar abuse, and she gave me a little cross, with the words 'God Loves You' on it. And she said, 'I want you to take this cross and put it on your mirror. And every time you see it I want you to say to yourself, "you are beautiful".' I couldn't do it, though – I still couldn't look in a mirror. But then as I was reading the Bible I came to the verse in Ecclesiastes 3, where it tells us God has made everything beautiful – 'He has made everything beautiful in its time' – and I thought, 'Does that mean me, too?' So I started looking in the mirror and trying to say what that woman had encouraged me to. 'You are beautiful. Everything God made is beautiful.' It was a struggle – I still struggle with it now – but day by day, I became more accepting of myself, and able to treat myself with kindness and love.

~~~

~27~

I wish I could tell you that this was the happy ending of my story: free of cancer, free of abuse, free to build my life and live it the way I'd dreamed of, back when I was trapped and controlled by David.

But it wasn't over, because his influence over my children was every bit as destructive as anything he'd ever done to me, and that only became more powerful after I left. He controlled them, and they were scared of him, and he still wanted to punish me.

When I first moved into my council house, he would send my son Luke to watch my whereabouts, so that at the beginning I hardly went out at all, unless it was to church. He sent messages through my son, saying, 'Tell her to come back and it'll be different.' I sent the message back: 'You tell him to get lost, I'll never be back,' and told Luke never to come to my home again with messages from him. For two years, I had to work at staying strong; not calling him. He'd still drive into my street sometimes, pumping his car horn, but there was a Neighbourhood Watch there, and they kept an eye out for me.

One time, much later, he phoned me. I don't know how he got the number; it must have been from one of the boys. His number was withheld, so I couldn't see who was calling, and I answered it.

'Elaine.' It was him. Just hearing his voice filled me with anger.

'What do you want?' I said.

'Ah now, Elaine, you're a Christian, you shouldn't be talking to me like that.'

'I don't want you calling me. If you phone me again I'll call the police.'

'No, no, no, you don't have to do that. I've been thinking, Elaine. For two years you've been away and you've stayed faithful to me, you've not had another man.'

'Faithful! I don't want you or any man. Do not phone me!'

'I was thinking, Elaine, I'll marry you now. And I'll buy you the most beautiful gold ring, the best gold ring ever.'

'Well, you can take your marriage, and you can take your ring and you can put them where the sun don't shine.'

He never bothered me on the phone again after that.

For another two years I lived on my own, and it seemed like David had completely backed off. Then my son Liam and my daughter Louise moved in. I was delighted – I thought they'd finally made the choice to be with me, and support me, rather than their dad. But it wasn't so: they were only there to monitor what I was doing and report back to David. He was still trapping and controlling me, though for a while I didn't know it.

~ ~ ~

~28~

The first incident came because of my work as a street pastor. David didn't know I was doing that until, one day, he saw a piece in the local paper about the work of street pastors, and there was a photograph of me. I was wearing the uniform, a cap saying 'Street Pastor' on it, the whole lot. Apparently he showed this to my son Luke, and said, 'That's your mum in that picture.' My son knew I was a street pastor, but had kept it a secret from his dad. He tried to deny it, but eventually had to admit it was me.

The next time I had a shift, when I came off the street at four in the morning, David followed me to the church, and starting banging on the church door. He was there for ages, shouting and bawling, saying, 'She's bringing shame on the family out there on the streets.' Shame! It was unbelievable: he was the violent, drug-dealing rapist, and I was bringing shame on his family by doing Christ's work! In the end one of my colleagues went to the church door and told him they'd call the police if he didn't leave.

The following weekend I was in the house and my eldest son, Matthew, sent me a text message. It didn't say anything particularly threatening, but I just had a feeling that something bad was about to happen. It was like the calm before the storm: I just sat there in the house through the evening with the blinds drawn, waiting and praying. Eventually I heard heavy vehicles outside, and when I peeked through the blinds I caught a glimpse of my son Matthew creeping around the outside of the house in a hoodie.

Then I heard Matthew's voice: 'Open the door!'

I ran to the bedroom and called the police, begging them to come quickly, and as I did I heard the front window smash.

The police got there too late – by the time they arrived Matthew and whoever else was with him had already done a lot of damage, smashing up the house, and they got away before the police arrived. The police took a statement from me, and took pictures of my sons from the house for identification.

I knew the kids were doing their father's bidding, and once again I felt scared and unsafe, wondering how far they would go to punish me. But I didn't have to wonder for long.

Around this time I'd made friends with a guy online. It was harmless, nothing sexual or romantic – I was just lonely and wanted someone to talk to. But Louise and Liam, who were still living with me, found out and told their dad, and once again, David went berserk. My older sons came straight to the house and confronted me, saying, 'You shouldn't be talking to any other men, you have a husband.' Well, for a start, David had never married me – but in any case, I was living on my own, and as far as I was concerned I could do what I liked. I told them this, and they started threatening me physically, throwing things around in the house and pushing me about, trying to get my phone off me so they could show their dad what I was writing to this guy

– but I kept my phone inside my clothes so they couldn't get it. Eventually they left, after trashing the house a bit more.

Later that day my friend Mairi called – she was an elderly lady from the church, who lived nearby with her husband, a retired minister – and said, 'Elaine, Jim and I think you should leave. We think they're going to kill you.'

The next day was a Sunday, and when I came out of church, I saw Matthew outside in his car. Mairi was giving me a lift into town, and I could see that Matthew was following us. As soon as Mairi dropped me off, Matthew jumped out of his car and grabbed me by the throat.

'You don't talk to other men online when you have a husband,' he snarled.

I said, 'I don't have a husband.'

Louise was with him, begging him to stop, not to hurt his mother.

'She's no mother of mine that would leave her husband and start speaking to some man online.'

I said, 'But Matthew, it's over. So it doesn't matter who I talk to; I'm free to talk to whoever I want.'

As he got back in his car and sped off, I saw that Mairi was still there, frozen with shock, watching through her windscreen.

Louise and I wandered around for a while after that, fending off abusive phone calls from David and my sons. Eventually we went back to the flat.

The next day, two police officers came.

'We believe your son assaulted you yesterday,' they said.

It turned out that Mairi had driven straight to the police to report what Matthew had done, and the incident had also been captured by a nearby CCTV camera.

'We want you to press charges against your son,' one of the officers said, but I couldn't. I knew it would only make things worse for me.

'Well, we're here if you change your mind,' he said.

At this point, Louise butted in, saying, 'My brother didn't do that.'

The police officer pointed out to her that there were witnesses and also CCTV evidence, and then took me aside, into the kitchen.

'What do you want to do?' he said.

'I don't know what to do, officer.'

'If you want to leave, we can help you to leave, but we don't think you're safe here where your children and their father can find you.'

I said, 'I know that. I'll think what to do.'

But it was already obvious what I had to do. Under their father's direction, my sons had smashed up my lovely house and destroyed my new life, and the only thing I could do was leave, because if I stayed it would never be over. I'd never be safe while they could still find me. That night, sobbing my heart out for everything I was about to lose, I packed a little holdall.

~ ~ ~

~29~

The next day, I was getting ready to leave.

'Where are you going?' asked Louise.

'I'm going to stay with a friend for a couple of days.'

'You can't do that.'

I said I could, and she started bawling and screaming at me, trying to physically stop me from walking out of the door. I managed to grab my holdall and walk out.

Louise followed close behind me and kept asking me where I was going. I said, 'Into the town,' just hoping I'd be able to get her off my tail before I reached the police station. As I was walking away with Louise following, I could hear her on her phone to her father, saying, 'It's mum. I think she's leaving. She's got a bag with her.' Eventually, I got to the entrance of the police station.

'Mum,' said Louise. 'If you go in there I'll never speak to you again.'

I went in and asked to see an officer who knew my situation. They took me into a little room and had another officer take Louise away in a police car so that I could leave in peace. I phoned my friend Sam, the wife of one of my cousins, who lived in a little village just north of Dundee, and Sam said if I could get to Aberdeen she'd pick me up from there. The police found the time of a bus going to Aberdeen from Elgin, took me to the bus stop and got me on the bus.

By the time I arrived in Aberdeen I was in a terrible state. I just couldn't believe I'd lost my home, just for talking to some stupid guy online, and I couldn't process the fact that my own children had done that to me.

Sam picked me up and took me to her house, but I could barely talk. For days, I couldn't eat at all, and my mind was a mess. I was still getting abusive text messages from my family – horrible, vicious, threatening stuff. I showed some of the text messages to Sam and she called the police, who came and took my phone away in case they needed it as evidence. At that point I lost all contact with my children.

A day or so later there was a phone call to Sam's house – she was married to my cousin, so in retrospect it was inevitable that eventually one of the family would find out where I was. They were threatening to come there and hurt me, so after only a week at Sam's, I moved south, into a Women's Aid refuge in Angus.

At that point, going into the refuge, I felt I'd lost everything. My kids, my friends, my home, my church, my phone and all my contact with the outside world. For the first time since my dad threw me out onto the street all those years ago, I was completely alone.

~~~

Part Seven

The Lord is my light and my salvation—
whom shall I fear?
The Lord is the stronghold of my life—
of whom shall I be afraid?

When the wicked advance against me
to devour me,
it is my enemies and my foes
who will stumble and fall.
Though an army besiege me,
my heart will not fear;
Though war break out against me,
even then I will be confident.

One thing I ask from the Lord,
this only do I seek:
that I may dwell in the house of the Lord
all the days of my life,

to gaze on the beauty of the Lord
and to seek him in his temple.

For in the day of trouble
he will keep me safe in his dwelling;
he will hide me in the shelter of his sacred tent
and set me high upon a rock.

Then my head will be exalted
above the enemies who surround me;
at his sacred tent I will sacrifice with shouts of joy;
I will sing and make music to the Lord.

Psalm 27:1–6

And I have promised to bring you up out of your misery in Egypt
into the land of the Canaanites . . . a land flowing with milk and
honey.

Exodus 3:17

~30~

After all the progress I'd made in my life, being back in refuge felt like a real low point. But I soon discovered that losing all contact with my family brought a peace to my life that I'd never known before. Soon I was offered a lovely council flat in Angus, and my life began to flourish again. My faith was growing ever stronger, as I could feel how God was transforming my life. Once again I was going to church and making friends – and this time, I was also really enjoying my own company. The pleasure of just coming home and being at peace with myself was wonderful.

I was still carrying all the scars and trauma, and I had nightmares most nights, but I could live with that.

I was just so thankful to God for bringing me through the darkness and saving me once again. As a Christian, I believed that Satan had tried to destroy me through the people he'd put in my life, but I was starting to see that God really did mean it all for good, just as in the story of Joseph, so that I could be the woman I am today.

That beautiful time in Angus was a glimpse of the land of milk and honey; the better life that God has in store for all of us, as He fulfils His purpose for our lives. But David still had people everywhere looking for me, and it was only eight months before one of his contacts sighted me in Angus and confronted me. The police were taking no chances this time: straight away, they moved me to the women's refuge in Dundee. And once again, I was isolated – exiled from home and a life I'd begun to love.

After growing up in institutions and then spending decades of my adult life imprisoned in the house by David, it had taken a lot for me to gain the confidence to branch out as a person. In Angus, I'd started to meet new kinds of people and try new things, and I could feel my life starting to expand with possibilities. But now, in Dundee, the paralysing fear I'd had since childhood gripped me again. Dundee was strange to me, and the whole world felt like a hostile place. I hardly ever went outside, and when I did I was always panicking and looking over my shoulder, thinking, 'who's coming to hurt me now?' I had some very dark days there. I cried a lot, begging the housing office to let me go back to Angus – but I knew they were right when they said I couldn't. There was no knowing what David would do this time.

This was a real bump in the road – but as always, the church was there for me. As the weeks went on, I spent nearly all my time with the church – barbecues, coffee mornings, bible study, prayer meetings, ladies' night. Services twice on a Sunday, and on weekday evenings. And during the day I helped out in the church when it was open to the public. Through the church I was able to rebuild my life once again. I loved my church.

I also started talking with women in the refuge about my life, and about God. So many of the women I got to know there wanted to go back to their abusers, as I had done so often in the past. They'd say to me, 'But what do you know? You wouldn't understand the life I've been through,' and I'd say, 'Well, I'm not in here for a holiday,' and I'd tell them something of my story. Sometimes after that, some of the women would ask me to pray for them, and I did.

In the refuge, I heard so many stories like my own, over and over again – about men who beat, and rape, and control – and I'd listen to these women, and my heart would be crying inside.

I love music – all music, but especially Christian music – and one day in the refuge I must have been playing my music louder than usual, trying to drown out dark, panicky thoughts. As I came out of my flat and started going down the stairs, a girl came out with a little toddler in a pram, and she said, 'Are you the lady that plays the loud music?'

I said, 'Yeah, I hope it's not bothering you.'

'Oh no,' she said, 'I don't mind it.' And as she kept standing there, I could tell she needed to talk.

'I'm in here because my husband rapes me,' she said, 'and he batters me. But you know the other night he phones me and he says, "Why don't you come home? I won't beat you anymore, it'll all be different." And you know what, Elaine? I miss the kisses and the hugs and the cuddles so much. I think I'm going to go back. What do you think I should do?'

I said, 'I'm not in a position to tell you what to do.'

So she said, 'What would you do?'

I said, 'I'll tell you this, I will never go back. You know, when you're involved with somebody like that and they're doing these things to you, they'll tell you they're sorry. And if you go back, it'll nice for a week or two, everything will be fine, then it all starts again. Then they'll be asking you who were you with, who were you talking to, what were you doing, and then the beatings start again. I can't tell you not to go back,' I said. 'I can't tell you to stay away. It's down to you. But if it was me, I wouldn't go back, because I understand that if you're with an abuser, it never stops.'

But that girl went back to her husband, and two weeks later, she was back in the refuge again.

My support worker encouraged me to go to meetings where there would be eight or ten women round a big table, and one of them would tell their story. The first time I went, it was a young girl called Danielle who was speaking. I'll never forget her: she was a beautiful girl, really lovely, and she had a little boy with her. She was telling her story about what the father of her son did to her – raped her, beat her, spied on her and stalked her – I could hardly bear to listen to it, it was so horrible. Then, after the meeting, we were talking and she said, 'I've met somebody else now and he's outside waiting for me. He's a soldier.' And off she went with this other guy – and I took one look at him, went back to the refuge and cried and cried for her, because it was just so obvious what was going to happen. It's so terribly difficult to break free from the spiral of abuse, and I know that I could only do it through the strength of God.

~ ~ ~

~31~

In 2017 I left the refuge in Dundee and moved up the coast to a lovely little fishing town, which is where I live now. By the time I moved there, I'd completely disconnected from everyone in my family, and I couldn't be contacted by them as nobody had my number.

But one day, as I was unpacking and organising things in my new home, I came across an old address book. It had all my children's phone numbers in, and I had to use all my strength not to give in to the temptation to call them. Instead, I phoned my eldest brother, James.

I dialled 141 first, because I still didn't want anyone to have my number, then I called. It was my sister-in-law Stella who picked up.

'It's Elaine,' I said. 'Look, I came across your number in an old book and to be honest I just want to speak to my brother.'

She said, 'Give me five minutes. Call me back in five minutes.'

So I waited, and after five minutes I called back. Stella said, 'Elaine, your brother here wants to talk to you.'

'Ok, great.'

'By the way, where are you, where do you live?'

'I'm sorry, I don't want to say where I am at the moment because of everything I've gone through.'

'Well,' she said, 'your brother wants to talk to you.'

When James came to the phone he was crying. He said, 'Elaine, why have you not called me before now? Why have you not texted me? All these years have gone by and I didn't know if you were dead or alive.'

'I couldn't,' I said, 'because I didn't know who was for me and who was against me. I was frightened.'

He said, 'Elaine, you must have known in your heart that I would never have told them where you were. Anyway, I'm glad you called, Sissy,' (he always called me Sissy) 'and I'm so that you're alive, because I didn't know. I thought you were dead.'

We talked for a while, and James kept asking where I was, and saying he wanted to see me.

'You know I'll never tell them that I've talked to you, I'll never tell them where you are or anything. Where do you live?'

'I don't want to say, I'm too scared.'

'Elaine, listen. I'm your brother. I know the life you've had with him. I wouldn't say anything. I just want to see you.'

'I'm afraid. But where are you right now, James? Where are you today?'

'I'm in Dundee. I'm in the Asda in Dundee.'

Well, that was a shock – my big brother was just along the road from the town where I lived! I was still scared, but just the thought of seeing my big brother and having him hold me – I wanted that so much. So I gave him my address and phone number.

The next week, he called to say he was in Dundee again, and he was going to come and visit me with Stella. I was so happy and excited! As soon as he walked in held me tight, and said, 'God, I just didn't know if you were dead or alive. I thought about you every day, and wondered what had happened to you – but it's just so good to know you're alive, and you're looking so well.'

James visited a couple more times, and we talked a lot. He told me that David had threatened him in the past, saying that if James ever found out where I was and didn't tell him, he'd have James killed. My big brother was frightened of David, and of my elder sons too, and I realised that just as I'd been scared of the consequences for me, he was taking a big risk in coming to see me as well.

We talked about Laura too, who I hadn't seen for years. When I first got free of David she used to come and visit me at my place in Elgin and tell me how proud she was of me for getting away and rebuilding my life. We were still close in our hearts, although in all the time I was with David he did everything he could to keep me apart from my siblings. James told me he'd spoken to Laura about me in the week, and told her we'd spoken and that I was well, but she'd received threats from David and my sons too, and was too scared to make contact with me herself. That was painful for me to hear, as I longed to see my little sister, but it was understandable, and I didn't want to put anyone in danger. I haven't seen James or Laura since then.

~ ~ ~

Part Eight

When we refuse to forgive, we are in disobedience to God's Word. We open a door for Satan to start all kinds of trouble in our lives. We hinder the flow of love toward others. Our faith is blocked and our prayers are hindered. We are miserable and lose our joy. Our attitudes are poisoned and we spew the poison onto everyone we meet. The price we pay to hang on to our bitter feelings is definitely not worth it. Unforgiveness does have devastating effects, so do yourself a favor . . . forgive!

Joyce Meyer, *Do Yourself a Favor . . . Forgive: Learn How to Take Control of Your Life Through Forgiveness*

For we know him who said, vengeance is mine; I will repay, says the Lord. And again, the Lord will judge his people.

Hebrews 10:30

~32~

Many of the people I've written about are no longer alive – and the first death, tragically, was that of my brother Jason. The time I ran away from the convent to find Jason at the boys' home was the last time I saw him, because David didn't let my brothers come to the house. But David knew him, and my eldest brother James was in touch with him from time to time. I knew Jason had married a girl in Aberdeen and had two sons, but he was an alcoholic, and his marriage ended because of his drinking. After that, he hung around with a bad crowd, just drinking and fighting.

It was one evening in 2001, back when I lived with David and the kids, when an item came on the TV news about a body that had been washed up on Portmahomack beach. They were appealing for anyone who could identify it to come forward. There was nothing in the news story to connect it to Jason, who didn't live anywhere near Portmahomack – but David kept saying he thought it was him. Eventually he phoned James, saying James should contact the police about identifying the body, because he thought it might be Jason. And it was. They could only identify him from his tattoos, he'd been so badly beaten. It turned out he'd been killed in a fight by some people he'd been drinking with: they beat him up and threw him into the river in Moray, and had washed all the way round to Portmahomack beach. By the time his body was found, it had been in the water six weeks. He was just forty-two, and the guy who did it got away, because none of the witnesses were prepared to testify against him. It was a sad end to a very sad life.

That same year, my mum came back. She was riddled with cancer, and knew she was dying – I think she just wanted to reconcile with her remaining children, as we were all she had. It was James she got in touch with first, and he contacted me.

I hadn't set eyes on my mum since that time she took us out from the orphanage to the Castle Restaurant in Inverness. The man she'd married, that quiet man with the watch, had work which took him all over the place, and she'd been living in England for most of the years in between. I was terrified at the thought of meeting her, because there had been no bond at all between us – but when I saw her, all I felt was love. I'd never really stopped wanting my mum, even though I hated her so much as a child. But I also wanted answers. I held her shrunken little hand and asked her, 'Why did you leave us like you did? Why did you do it?' But instead of her apologising, somehow it was me. Deep inside, I was still that little girl who blamed herself.

For nearly two years I spent time with her, as she was dying, but she never really opened up to me. She was a very shaky, nervous woman, and being with her was difficult and strange. Eventually, shortly before she died, she said, 'You don't know the life that I had. I couldn't stay.' But she wouldn't say any more than that, and I never told her what my life was like either – I was too ashamed of the way David treated me.

James told me that he remembered getting up for a pee one night and seeing our dad trying to strangle her in the bathroom. But I still didn't feel I truly understood why she abandoned me and Laura as tiny children. There was also the story he told me of my dad's father offering her money to leave, which always niggled at me. I think James knew more about that part of the past than he said – he never really opened up either, although he'd give me little nuggets of information when I asked.

I was already a committed Christian by the time Mum came back, and I knew I had to forgive her, painful as it was. When I sat with her, she used to say, 'There's such a peace about you, Elaine,' and I'd tell her about God's love, and about salvation. And eventually, before she died, she was Born Again. The thought that she was saved at the end makes me happy, as I know one day I'll see her again.

For Laura it was harder. She was younger, and perhaps had been even more traumatised than me, and she was full of bitterness and hatred. She'd never sought out any help over the years, whereas I'd had support from the church. Laura thought she could be strong and handle it all herself as an adult, and of course she couldn't – nobody can. So when Mum came back, she didn't cope with it at all. I talked with Laura about God too, and about forgiveness, and at the very end, after Mum had died and just before her funeral, Laura dropped a letter she'd written into the casket. I asked her, 'Did you do it?'

'Yeah,' she said. 'I've forgiven her. I've let it go.'

Our Dad died next, although I didn't see him towards the end. He'd reappeared from time to time when I lived with David – he was living in a housing estate in Inverness, but David would never take me to visit. Again, it was James who told me he was getting ill. He was in hospital with a heart attack, then had cancer, and then – very weirdly – ended up in Scotscraig, the orphanage Laura and I had grown up in, which had been turned into a care home. He died there.

I have one picture of my dad – a photo of a photo, from his gravestone at the cemetery, and I still get a pain in my heart whenever I look at it. How could he not have protected us and kept us safe? Why was he never there to guide me and lead me through my life? In the picture, he's around sixty. I know he was an alcoholic, and he doesn't look as though he had a happy life at all. You can see it in his eyes.

~~~

~33~

When I was in the women's refuge in Dundee I was given a lot of counselling, and at one point, my counsellor mentioned the possibility of compensation for the abuse I'd suffered while I was in the Scottish care system. So I told my whole story to a panel, and described how the abuse I'd suffered as a child had affected the rest of my life, which of course included my relationship with David. At this point the police became involved again, as they were called to verify my account – checking their reports for the times I was beaten, the times the police were called to the house, and so on. And as a result of that, the decision was taken to try and bring the perpetrators to justice. They'd wanted to arrest Ada Stevenson, but she was already dead by this point, and they decided to arrest David. From my perspective, this wasn't about punishing David – I'd already forgiven him – but it was part of the justice process that I was involved in. Officers were due to go to Elgin and arrest him in December 2017, but he died just before they got there. And in a way I wasn't sorry about that. Arresting David was the necessary response to all the evidence that had been given in support of my compensation claim, but I was glad he was spared from living out the rest of his days in prison.

My youngest daughter Louise told me that in the hospital he was always watching and waiting, asking, 'Who's that, who's that?' whenever the door opened or closed, hoping that it would be me. She told me that as he was dying, he apologised, saying to her, 'Find your mother. Don't hate her. I'm sorry for what I've done to her. I loved her, I shouldn't have hurt her. And I'm sorry for what I've done to you all. I was too hard on every one of you.'

He repented at the end, and asked God for forgiveness. The Bible does say that whoever calls on God's name will be saved, and tells us that God is merciful, and if you repent of your sins and believe, then you're promised eternal life. And David had certainly been to enough funerals in his time to know that he had to get right with God in the end.

When Louise told me about his apology to me, and about him seeking forgiveness from God, I found it really hard to deal with. He can't have loved me, after all – love doesn't do what he did for all those years. I asked him once, after I'd left, 'Why did you do all those things to me?' and he said, 'To teach you a lesson.' I still don't understand what he meant by that, but I do now believe his apology was genuine – and eventually, after a lot of prayer, I've been able to accept it, and feel glad that he's in Heaven and not in Hell.

~ ~ ~

~34~

It's hard to practise forgiveness, but that's what God expects of each of us, and He forgives us in turn. God tells us that there is forgiveness for every single person who will take it. It's hard to choose to love, instead of clinging to our hurts, but Christ can remove the hardness in our hearts and set us free. Forgiveness is necessary, because the alternative is bitterness – and if bitterness takes root, it poisons our lives.

For me, forgiveness is an ongoing process. It's taken me a long time, and it's still a choice I have to deliberately make. Every day I pray to God to give me the strength to walk in forgiveness. I've had a lot of counselling too, and it's still available to me any time I need it: if I find myself brooding on the terrible harms that were done to me, and spiralling into dark thoughts, I can pick up the phone to the medical centre and get help. Without that combination of Christian faith and professional support, I think my journey towards fully healing would be a lot harder.

Forgiveness doesn't mean justifying the actions of rapists, wife-beaters and child-abusers: it doesn't mean jumping back into their circle. Forgiveness means the ability to move on; to walk away. I believe we're all sinners saved by the Spirit. We've all fallen short of God's glory. So for me, forgiveness means thinking, 'Well, my mum and dad were the parents God gave me. They were wounded and damaged in their own ways, and couldn't have fully known what they were doing.'

Most importantly, for me, forgiveness means freeing myself from the hurt of the past, so that I can accept the call that God has placed on me, and focus fully on the future. I know that God was with me through all the pain, and He loved me and cared for me and kept me strong. He walked me through it and brought me out the other side to the place I am now, and I'm just so thankful for that. I know that everything I suffered God will use for good, and that He has a plan for the rest of my life.

This side of Heaven, we all have our bumps in the road; painful things happen to all of us, as well as good things. And sometimes it seems like there's far more pain than good. But when I get to Heaven, I know I'll live forever on the other side, happy.

And in the meantime, I just want to help others to get there.

So whatever suffering you're experiencing right now, I hope this book helps you to believe that there will be a way through for you, no matter how long it takes, and that the struggle to get there will be worth it. Because if I can forgive and heal after a whole lifetime of abuse, then maybe you can, too.

~ ~ ~

'For I know the plans I have for you,' declares the Lord, 'plans for good and not for evil, plans to give you hope and a future. Then you will call on me and come and pray to me, and I will listen to you. You will seek me and find me when you seek me with all your heart. I will be found by you,' declares the Lord, 'and will bring you back from captivity.'

Jeremiah 29:11–14

AFTERWORD: JANUARY 2022

As I write this final chapter, I've just come back from spending Christmas with my children and grandchildren. Yes, you read that right: Christmas with my children and grandchildren!

Since David's death, we've begun rebuilding a relationship. As adults, they are now aware of how much their father hurt them, and how destructive his controlling influence on them was. They're also more able to recognise the pain I suffered, and each of my children has apologised to me in recent years. It's still tricky, though: I have a lot of anxiety and trust issues, and there are a lot of gaps to bridge, after decades of estrangement. But the life I want is one with my children in it – I long for us to have a close and easy relationship, and we've made a good start. We've sung and danced and eaten and laughed together, and I've been shopping for clothes and make-up with my daughter Louise – it's a beautiful thing to have a daughter to tell you how to do your make-up! I often feel sad when I think about how much of their lives I've missed, but Louise says, 'Mum, don't worry about that anymore – we'll make new memories.'

I still live in the town I moved to when I left the refuge in Dundee, and it's a place I love. Although I sometimes struggle with the after-effects of trauma, my life is overflowing with goodness – more than I ever could have imagined. I have my faith, my friends, my freedom, my family and my future. I have my physical health. And since Christmas, I even have a little dog – a gorgeous wee Shih Tzu called Scooby.

Having been plagued by financial troubles and serious debt ever since I left David, I've now been awarded compensation – it's not riches by any means, but it's enough to keep me secure, and I'm using some of it to finally learn how to drive. And just recently, I was asked by the staff at the Women's Aid refuge if I would consider volunteering there to help counsel other women, which is something I'm really keen to do.

There are gaps, of course. I lost forty-two years of my life to David and I don't know if I'll ever have a loving relationship with a man, although I do know that if God means me to be with a man, it'll be someone of His choosing. And there are still the two sons I was forced to give up for adoption when I was a teenager, whom I've never met. One of them, Robbie, was taken to Australia, and I've spoken to him once on the phone, but I don't know if I'll ever see him face to face.

But now these are my only sadnesses, in the midst of everything God has done to transform my life. Writing this book has been the beginning of something new and exciting for me – the start of my life's true purpose, and my mission as a Christian. And I just can't wait to see where it takes me next!

Thank you for reading my story.

With love and blessings,

Elaine.

ACKNOWLEDGEMENTS

Grateful thanks to Sam Boyce for helping me to write this book, to Future Pathways who made it all possible, and to Diana Stewart for all her support, prayers and encouragement.

Elaine Rose lives on the north-east coast of Scotland, and worships at her local evangelical church. This is her first book.

Printed in Great Britain
by Amazon